I0167386

WAR
OF THE POETS

A.D.PADGETT

"All poet's fail. That is
why there is
always room for
another."
Humbert Wolfe *Modern Verse*

Published by
ADP Publishing

First Published 2015
Copyright Anthony Padgett 2015

ISBN 978-0-9572919-3-5

INDEX

INTRODUCTION

Perhaps more than any other vocation, the poet's is full of wrangling and jockeying for position. The financial rewards are few and rare, yet the competition is intense. Warlike.

Herein are some of the most entertaining and key literary wars waged between 1919 and 1939, constructed from fragments of a broken landscape of letters and biographies.

The protagonists and antagonists include; T.S. Eliot, Wyndham Lewis, Siegfried Sassoon, W.H. Auden, Edith & Osbert & Sacheverell Sitwell, Roy Campbell, Cecil Day-Lewis, Stephen Spender, Wilfred Owen, Robert Graves, Rebecca West, Vita Sackville-West, Humbert Wolfe, Virginia & Leonard Woolf, Noel Coward, George Moore, Victor Gollancz, Pamela Frankau, Thomas Hardy, John Gawsworth, T.E. Lawrence, James Joyce, Nancy Cunard and Stephen Tennant.

Many were born in the 1880s, e.g. Wyndham Lewis, Humbert Wolfe, Siegfried Sassoon, Edith Sitwell & T.S. Eliot. They were in the Modernist and the Bloomsbury Groups who attacked the nostalgic Georgian poets and their love of early twentieth century rural England.

And what of their tactics. Some, like Rebecca West, criticised a person's character. Others, like Humbert Wolfe criticised a person's work. Others still, like Wyndham Lewis, criticised both.

My remit is not to see if the pen was mightier than the sword (or rather the gun). Nor is it to judge who won the many wars of the poets (though as a sculptor and relative of Humbert Wolfe I must declare a vested interest). Take the literary skirmish between Humbert Wolfe and Siegfried Sassoon. Sassoon attacked Humbert but both could be said to have won. Sassoon is remembered for his war poems and won the war of the soldier in history and death. And Humbert was a best seller of the 1920s and won the war of the lover in the moment.

I prefer that you, dear reader, decide on your winners and losers, or just allow yourself to be entertained without needing to judge.

And to an extent all poets lost as the Great War marked the beginning of the end of their cultural dominance. In their earlier world they had read and published each other and appointed themselves the learned greats that the public should love. They had been the winners.

These poets were not democratic and weren't judged on sales because they could live off their inheritances. They were both dictators and entertainers. Masters over the reader but needy of the readers' praise. However, when T.S. Eliot became the leader of this elite he destroyed notions of the English poet. He was the American, who fulfilled British culture whilst American popular culture drowned it out with cinema. The end of the poets was the victory of Hollywood and Eliot was its Trojan Horse, letting in the Cuckoo who destroyed the cultural nest.

And whilst cinema ransacked the popularity of the poets it also harnessed their power as writers of wartime propaganda, in a heady combination of cinema, jingoism and art. Perhaps the winners of the war of the poets were those who supported Britain and the allies as many poets had initially supported Hitler and Franco and others Stalin and the Communists.

NOTE ON SOURCES

To mimic the voice of one genius is presumptuous but to mimic the voices of two dozen genii is preposterous. So I present stories and anecdotes by way of sayings and incidents actually published by the characters or their biographers.

In this complex jigsaw I have not invented any information. Some stories and connections have, however, been simplified for the sake of comprehension and entertainment. Too much information would kill the stories. So some characters have been omitted from situations. Some stories have also been omitted as not enough information exists to bring them to life.

Quotes have been used in line with "Fair Use" for purposes of criticism and review of the works and lives of the characters.

To enable the stories to flow I have not put references in the text (as this would make it unreadable) but list published sources at the back of this book. And I wish to respectfully thank the authors.

I use surnames both out of respect and because using Christian names would make the relationships harder to follow. However, for Edith, Osbert and Sacheverell Sitwell I use Christian names to avoid confusion. The same is the case for Virginia and Leonard Woolf and Humbert Wolfe. Hopefully this does not create an unfair sense of familiarity.

A brief biography of the characters and chapters they are in (to help readers track of the complex relationships) is at the back of the book.

So imagine sitting with me in my study. Books piled high beside me and a bookcase full behind me. Occasionally I will pull one from the shelf to burnish a quote. Now, please make yourself comfortable and have a drink whilst we begin…

Ch 1 : *BLAST* BEFORE THE WAR (1914)

GEORGIAN POETRY

In the 1910s the Georgian poets were fashionable. They avoided the words and themes of Victorian and Edwardian sentimentality and aimed to be simple, natural and pastoral and took their name from the monarch at the time, King George V, and one of their meeting places was Harold Monro's Poetry Bookshop.

These Left Wing literary rebels waged Literary warfare with the 'stuffed shirts' of the establishment, however, in 1913 Modernist writers like Ezra Pound and Wyndham Lewis were beginning their own campaigns. Pound had high hair, stubble and a goatee beard. His shirt was open at the top with tie pulled loose gave him the appearance of a bohemian worker. He was volatile and his Imagist poetry did not need to rhyme but followed an inner music. Pound had been foreign editor of *Poetry* a Chicago magazine that became the organ of new writers.

In 1914, the Georgian poet Lascelles Abercrombie published an essay urging a return to the poet William Wordsworth in a search for true values. So Pound sent a letter challenging Abercrombie to a duel, claiming that: "Stupidity carried beyond a certain point becomes a public menace." Abercrombie, as the challenged party, had the right to choose weapons and when he learned that Pound was a skilful fencer he suggested that they throw at each other the unsold copies of their books. Although this "duel" did not occur it marked the beginning of the slow demise of the Georgian poets.

ROTHENSTEIN PAINTS LEWIS

But before this demise there came a revolution in art, spearheaded in Britain by the artist and man of letters Wyndham Lewis. Lewis was shy, secretive and temperamental. He was an outsider who created an aura of villainy, wearing tall black hats and a huge black cape. He had been educated at Rugby Public school but was asked to leave for transforming his study into a painter's studio. He saw English training as a system of deadening feeling and believed intuition was the only way to express reality.

Lewis was introduced to the older, traditional artist, William Rothenstein whilst still at the Slade School of Art in London. Rothenstein did 2 portraits of Lewis and encouraged Lewis writing: "I had known Lewis as a handsome youth, adventurous, but uncertain of direction. I now discovered a formidable figure, armed and armoured, like a tank, ready to cross any country, however rough and hostile, to attack without formal declaration of war .... Lewis was a master of controversy; with no social or party ties, ... He was not out against the Philistine, but the literary and artistic gunman, an enemy as well armed as himself. I admired his bold demeanour, and though I re-membered the talent he showed when, as a youngster, he sent me his sonnets, I was astonished at his range as a writer. ... I hold him to be the most forceful and intellectual of English experimenters."

Lewis' returning compliments were more muted; "Rothenstein was a brilliant artist and a small man with balding head and round glasses. Whose intelligence and keen sense of humour struck you before his very good dress sense."

"Sir William Rothenstein was until last year principal of the South Kensington Schools and in that capacity irradiated his intelligence over the back areas of England, and many a poor fellow now can draw a cow-or, to be more accurate, teach another fellow how to draw a cow-who otherwise would have remained completely unresponsive to the presence of that quadruped. What it was possible for a man to do, Rothenstein did. You can't make a silk purse out of a sow's ear, and the times are not propitious for folk-art." Lewis thought that; "Rothenstein's brilliant services as an educationalist have rather over-shadowed his achievement as a painter and draughtsman. This great wit, for he is the last of the wits, is quite a different man when he paints. No sign there of the flashing intelligence.

He becomes a humble workman, fumbling almost in his grim sincerity."

Rothenstein was always a welcome visitor at his studio, "because so witty. I gave him one of my best drawings of that time. This is how it happened. He came in one day just before his brother turned up and made me very conceited by the generous praise he bestowed upon all he saw. One thing-a drawing in ink-the best small thing I had, he asked me to put aside. He must *possess* that, he said, if he could, and at once I put it aside. That was for *him*. After a few weeks I sent it round to his house. Meeting him in Church Street one day he bore down upon me all brilliantly lighted up, his eyes shining, uttering an apology six yards away about this drawing which brought a blush to my cheek. If one artist could not give a drawing to another! I exclaimed-for, of course, I had given him that. He should have understood. And peering brightly up into my face he thanked me as only he is able to thank: 'There is a saying,' he said, 'in the bible, *Blessed is he who gives and blessed is he who receives!* So I will accept it without hesitation.'"

POUND MEETS LEWIS

In 1912-13 Pound and Lewis met at the Vienna Cafe, a coffee house and gathering place for European emigres. Lewis was seated in a red plush chair at a table with a few other Englishmen. Pound had recently arrived in London and approached him as if he was a panther, "tense and wary, without speaking or smiling: showing one is not afraid of it, [but] inwardly awaiting hostile action." And Lewis saw Pound as a "cowboy songster" and a Jew in disguise.

It was a few years before they trusted each other and they realized how much they had in common. Traits like infuriating their acquaintances and enjoying offending the impeccable manners of the English.

Lewis exhibited a series of semi-abstract drawings based on Shakespeare's *Timon of Athens* at the second

Postimpressionist show, in 1912. The black and white warriors wore helmeted masks and were fragmented by overlapping planes. Pound commented that they showed what the play exposed: the "fury of intelligence baffled and shut in by a circumjacent stupidity."

Pound wrote, in the magazine *The Egoist*, with hatred for the stupidity of the British, who would not accept the new art Lewis was championing: "The "man in the street" cannot be expected to understand the "*Timon*" at first sight. Damn the man in the street, once and for all, damn the man in the street who is only in the street because he hasn't intelligence enough to be let in to anywhere else, and who does not in the least respect himself for being in the street, any more than an artist would respect himself for being hung in the Royal Academy. But the man .... who has some sort of hunger for life, some restlessness for a meaning, is willing to spend six months, any six months, in a wilderness of doubt if he may thereby come to some deeper understanding; to some emotion more intense than his own; to some handling of life more competent than his own fumbling about the surface. So it is amply worth while taking half a year to get at the "Timon," fumbling about, looking at Matisse and Cezanne and Picasso, and Gauguin and Kandinsky, and spoiling sheet after sheet of paper in learning just how difficult it is to bring forth a new unit of design."

BLAST

Lewis' paintings spear-headed the new "Vorticist" movement and had a hard, geometric energetic style. And his stories and caricatures were as hard and brutal. Lewis' main character of his acclaimed 1914 novel *Tarr* (whom he resembled) was an isolated figure with a persecution mania and "no social machinery" and came across as being pretentious when trying to be amiable.

In 1914 Lewis produced a combination of his artistic and literary interests in a puce coloured folio with "*BLAST*" in diagonal across the front and back. It combined his painting and writing interests and included a Vorticist Maifesto by Pound and Lewis. It began with a list of "blasted" and of "blessed".

The "blessed" included James Joyce and Lewis' collaborators. And he "blasted" included Virginia Woolf of the Bloomsbury Group. This group had no shared style or subject but were part of an upper-middle-class seeking cultural change. Many were Cambridge educated, conscientious objectors and atheists. They had a sexual and social candour but they were not Socialists and were not at ease with lower classes. Pound felt that the Bloomsbury writers were clogged down with stuffy English notions of class and called them "Bloomsbuggers".

Pound included twelve poems in *BLAST*. The erotic imagery of one of which almost prevented the publication of the whole magazine. *Fratres Minores* satirized the woolly approach to love favoured by latter-day Romantic poetry:

> With minds still hovering above their testicles
> Certain poets here and in France
> Still sigh over established and natural fact
> Long since fully discussed by Ovid.
> They howl. They complain in delicate and exhausted metres
> That the twitching of three abdominal nerves
> Is incapable of producing a lasting Nirvana.

BLAST also included fiction by Rebecca West and others. Lewis was the first person to publish her fiction. She was invited to participate partly because she had supported Lewis' first book tour of *Tarr*. Her contribution, *Indissoluble Matrimony,* was a melodramatic story of sexual antagonism that had been turned down by *The English Review* and *The Blue Review*.

West was a small lady with bob-length dark hair. Her small eyes, nose and mouth were all poised for the right moment to speak. She was as plain as her make-up, her dress sense and her speaking. Similarly her simple cardigans covered pretty blouses and dresses, but these were adorned with a long pendant that betrayed her exotic nature.

Indissoluble Matrimony contained images of violence and militancy in keeping with the *BLAST* manifestos: "They were broken into a new conception of life... And those who were gentle by nature and shrank from the ordained brutality were betrayers of their kind, surrendering the earth to the seed of their enemies." But although the main characters eventually fall into "a brawling blackness in which whirled a vortex", *Indissoluble Matrimony* was not a real Vorticist story as it was still conventional in style.

Lewis' own experimental *Enemy of the Stars* had the abstraction, iconoclasm and vitality of Vorticism. It divided the prose into isolated sentences without conventional syntax or linear narratives. Lewis hoped to purge his writing of time-oriented form for a disconnected prose full of bizarre imagery, sudden scene-changes and fragmented episodes. Technology and primitivism combined in Lewis' turbulent imagination, as he waited for Armaggedon.

And so when in 1914 Pound exclaimed "Artists are the antennae of the race" he had in mind Lewis. And this vision fit with the political tensions presaging the First World War.

THE AMERICAN ENGLISHMAN

Another key collaborator for Pound was Thomas Stearns Eliot. Pound was the first in England to show any interest in Eliot's poem *The Love Song of J. Alfred Prufrock*. Harold Monro, at the Georgian Poetry Bookshop, had dismissed it as "absolutely insane". But Pound was astonished by it and said that it was "the best poem I have yet had or seen from an American." Pound was amazed because Eliot; "has actually trained himself and modernized himself on his own."

They first met in 1914 and had tea among the stacks of books and papers in Pound's triangular study in Kensington. He showed Eliot Lewis' *Timon of Athens* drawings and promoted Vorticism to a tactfully noncommittal Eliot. Eliot was encouraged by Pound's enthusiasm for his work. Eliot had been in Germany, on a travelling fellowship from Harvard, pursuing a graduate degree in epistemology, but had to leave because of the outbreak of the war. He was a tall, sleek, impeccably dressed figure who was also a nervous and anxious young man. He was careful about his speech and details of what he said. And was also self-mocking.

Eventually Lewis also met Eliot at Pound's sitting room in early 1915. Pound introduced the tall, clerical Eliot to Lewis, but Eliot was reserved and quiet. So Pound began to speak in a hill-billy accent, promising Lewis that Eliot was livelier than he seemed. Lewis recalled the meeting: "This very small room, in which Mr. Eliot had alighted, and in which he sat placidly smiling, was, allowance made for the comic side of Ezra's manic herding of talent, a considerable place."

Each had spent their childhood in America and shared a belief that democracy would erode all cultural standards. Lewis included Eliot's *Prelude* and *Rhapsody on a Windy Night*, in a second number of *BLAST* and this was Eliot's first real publication anywhere. He also considered printing Eliot's undergraduate *Bullshit* and *The Ballad of Big Louise*, but then remembered the difficulty he had over Pounds profanities in the first issue of *BLAST*.

Lewis said of Eliot "his face would be haggard, he would seem at his last gasp.... To ask him to lie down for a short while at once was what I always felt I ought to do. However, when he had taken his place at a table, given his face a dry wash with his hands, and having had a little refreshment, Mr. Eliot would rapidly shed all resemblance to the harassed and exhausted refugee, in flight from some Scourge of God."

Eliot was to call Lewis "the most fascinating personality of our time". With "the thought of the modern and the energy of the cave-man." Eliot's self- restraint and conventionality hid a cold fury that was easily provoked. And whilst Eliot was preoccupied with reaching down to the savage dark unconscious nature within himself Lewis didn't have a Vorticist literary group for him to join so Eliot gravitated to Virginia Woolf's Bloomsbury Group. And it was her husband, Leonard Woolf, who saw clearly that the preceding decade of political and social change, where "it seemed as though human beings might really be on the brink of becoming civilized", was now over and it was the "end of hope."

Ch 2 : WAR (1914-1918)

The Georgians loved the English countryside but were based in the city. They were parodied as fake pastoralists and dubbed "lark lovers" or "weekenders". The harsh reality of World War I brought a revolt against them and their poetry. However, they still had many supporters, including many of the young War Poets who were dubbed Neo-Georgians. Included in this small army were Siegfried Sassoon, Robert Graves, Osbert Sitwell and his brother Sacheverell Sitwell.

Siegfried Sassoon had been cricketer, huntsman and self-published poet who joined the Royal Welsh Fusiliers as an officer, and was sent to France in November 1915. Sassoon was tall, lean and agile. His father was a rich Persian Jew who married into a British Anglican family and he had a strong jaw, wide mouth, dark eyes and arched nostrils that gave him the appearance of a warhorse or a bird of prey. He spoke slowly, in well spoken English, as if the words pained him. His large hands wandered until fired with emotion and then he would clench his knuckles and breathe hard.

He became fanatically brave, seeking revenge on the Germans for his brother Hamo's death at Gallipoli in 1915 and for the death of his friend, David Thomas. His extreme actions earned him the nickname "Mad Jack" though he was also known amongst the soldiers as "the Pen Pusher".

During July 1916, when Sassoon was twenty-nine, he met Robert Graves, who was nine years younger. Graves was also tall, inward and intense. He was attractive with large cheekbones, full lips, bent nose (appearing broken), grey eyes and thick, unruly black curly hair. Graves immediately liked Sassoon but not his sentimental and rhetorical war poetry. They become close friends, although Graves was always giving Sassoon opinions without being asked. And Graves dressed badly and sloppily as an officer. They discussed living and travelling together if they survived the war. They would exchange letters about their attraction towards other men.

Sassoon had already cultivated similar friends whom he introduced to Graves.

In July 1916 the British hoped for a breakthrough at the Battle of the Somme but it ended in failure. The heavy rain turned the trenches into mud baths. And soldiers were forced to advance out of these trenches into German machine-gun fire. A quarter of a million soldiers died.

The Royal Welsh Fusiliers were in reserve just behind the front lines when on 20 July 1916, just before he turned 21, a German shell exploded behind Graves and he was hit by fragments of shrapnel. Despite the wounds he was partly conscious. When he lost consciousness all expected he would die. An official letter was sent to notify his parents of his death and a report of his death was carried by *The Times*. Sassoon also wrote a poem to his memory called *To His Dead Body*.

And then Graves was found breathing and miraculously regained consciousness, though in great pain. After ten days in a field hospital he returned to England where he recovered from a damaged right lung, though he suffered shell shock for the rest of his life. Graves joked about his reported death and *The Times* offered to publish a retraction for free.

Sassoon was also wounded and returned to England. He had been decorated with the Military Cross for bravery and said of his decoration. "At first I thought of refusing it, as I was so violently, passionately opposed to the way the war had been conducted, and indeed to the war itself. Then I had second thoughts. I wish it had been a V.C. (Victoria Cross) it would give poets a tremendous leg up. But it would take a lot of living up to."

Eventually, disgusted by the loss of life, he defied public opinion and the authorities by throwing away his medal and sending out a statement calling for the end of the war and refusing to fight any more battles. He was still in the army and his action could have led to his court martial, which he wanted for the publicity it would bring to his argument.

Graves was stunned at Sassoon's public refusal to fight and felt that pacifists were influencing him and ruining him. So

Graves lied to Sassoon that his statement would not gain publicity. And to extricate Sassoon from imprisonment and possible execution (that refusing to fight and encouraging others to desert would entail) he persuaded Sassoon to appear before a medical board and argue that he was suffering from shell shock.

Graves was crying when he made his presentation to the medical board. But the appearance was successful. Sassoon's poetry was already famous and to avoid damaging effects the authorities dealt with his protest by treating it as the result of a nervous breakdown.

Sassoon was sent to Craiglockhart War Hospital near Edinburgh where he was treated by doctor William Rivers. Rivers was also treating Graves' friend Peter Johnstone to "cure" him of his homosexuality. Graves followed Johnstones path and in 1917 Sassoon received apologies from Graves for his engagement to a painter, Nancy Nicholson, who was from a well known cultured family. Sassoon angrily noted the letter of betrayal in his diaries. And Graves later demanded that Sassoon accept his change in sexual orientation as well as asking Sassoon for money. Robert Graves and Nancy Nicholson married in early 1918.

But Sassoon found new friends out of the situation. He met the poet Wilfred Owen at Craiglockhart. Owen was impeccable in uniform, with close shaven hair and a moustache on his young face. His strong and kind eyes were tired and aged by the horrors of war. He admired Sassoon's work, though his own poems were more basic, sentimental sonnets. They became close friends and Sassoon encouraged Owen to experiment, and then showed and impressed Graves with Owen's writings.

Ch 3 : *WHEELS* (1915 – 1921)

Sassoon found other literary friends even more receptive to Owen's work. The Sitwells – Osbert, Sacheverell and Edith.

Osbert and Sacheverell had both gone to Eton and were now officers in the Grenadier-Guards. They had rosy complexions and Osbert, the older of the two, was plump with large eyes and a down-pointing, Roman nose over a small chin. He dressed smartly whether in uniform or a top hat and evening wear as the gent around town. Osbert fought but by the time Sacheverell had completed his training the war was over. Sachie was slimmer and with a straighter nose. He dressed like his older brother though not quite as slick and exacting.

Their sister Edith was the eldest, though unlike her brothers, she was not wealthy. Although first born, she did not have the larger inheritance as was traditional for a woman in that time. None-the-less it was Edith who was Queen Bee, surrounding herself with new proteges. She lived in London with her former governess at 22 Pembridge Mansions, a rented Bayswater Flat, instead of living in the more fashionable Chelsea. She was 6' tall, with a curved spine, a pale faced, lank-hair and a long curved nose. But she had a flair for promoting herself as enigmatically stylish with infallibile taste. Her poetry was experimental with bizarre and unusual rhythms and verse forms. It contained a free association of classical, biblical, mythical and personal childhood imagery.

In 1916 Edith, along with the wealthy young social rebel Nancy Cunard, published *Wheels* an annual anthology of poetry. They took themselves seriously in their revolt against the "verbal deadness" of Georgian poetry but the magazine was sour and flippant and of interest to only a small group of intellectuals.

Osbert, Sacheverell and Edith saw each other as geniuses and *Wheels* was their vehicle to show this. Seven of Nancy Cunard's poems were also published in *Wheels*. They were the first poems that Nancy published but were not favourably received. The anthology also included poets like Wyndham Lewis.

Osbert also founded his own quarterly review *Art and Letters* 1917-1920 to which Lewis was a regular contributor and work was contributed by Siegfried Sassoon and Robert Graves.

Sassoon found Osbert charming and had met him in 1917 through a mutual friend. Osbert admired Sassoon's principled stand, more than his poetry, but did not take a similar stance. And the Sitwell's contempt for the Georgians made Sassoon feel old-fashioned. However, they were from similar backgrounds and talked to each other with freedom, against a largely hostile world.

Sassoon sent Osbert an advance copy of *The Old Huntsman* a collection of his subversive war poetry. "I hope you'll not be disappointed", he wrote. "It is highly suitable for people of a funereal disposition and should have a great success among undertakers." Osbert's work had similar themes and only their style differed.

In July 1917, Sassoon introduced Osbert to his new poetic talent. "Have you met Wilfred Owen, my little friend, whose verses were in the *Nation* recently?"…"He is so nice, and shy, and fervent about poetry, which he is quite good at and will do very well one day."

Osbert met Owen a few weeks later and Osbert was "not to frighten him". They soon established that they had a common delight in "the company of our friends, a love of books, and a hatred of modern war." Owen and Sassoon went with Osbert to hear Mrs Gordon Woodhouse play her harpsichord and then went back to Osbert's house for a "sumptuous tea which culminated in – was it raspberries and cream? And ices of incredibly creamy quality." The friendship throve and Owen wrote regularly from camp.

The next year Owen told Osbert that in July 1918 that he broke out of camp to order a 1917 copy of *Wheels* at a Scarborough bookshop. The shop assistant had no knowledge of the publication so Owen protested so loudly that "the Young Lady loudly declared she knew all along that I was "Osbert himself". This caused consternation throughout the crowded shop; but I got the last laugh by – "No, Madam, the book is by a friend of mine, Miss Sitwell.""

Sassoon had also presented Owen to Edith who shared the sense of disgust at the war. Edith wrote "Nothing will ever make me believe that war is either a good thing or a wise thing, or that there can be any possible justification for sending out some millions of men for the avowed purpose of killing each other." War was such a "beastly thing."

Owen wished to "help with the ammunition" to contribute a poem to the 1918 collection of *Wheels* if it would continue the crusade against the war and "go on the caterpillar wheels of Siegfried's Music Hall Tank?" which Sassoon wished would drive down the music hall stalls to make sure that there were no more jokes "to mock the riddled corpses" of soldiers.

A few days later Owen was sent back to France. Then, a week before the Armistice, the end of the war, he was killed with no book of his work yet published.

Osbert wrote to the poet's mother, from the hospital where he was recovering from an almost lethal bout of Spanish influenza. "I was so dreadfully sorry to hear about Wilfred, ... I can't tell you how much I feel for you – and how personally we all feel the loss."

Owen's poems would appear in the following year's collection of *Wheels* compiled by Edith. She was the first to publish a body of Owen's work and had wanted to prepare his manuscripts for publication and gain the credit, presenting him as her discovery. But Sassoon had taken Owen's mud bespattered manuscripts and prepared them for publication himself, as Owen had been his friend. Edith had already been working on some of them and was upset not to do the complete job.

Osbert celebrated the posthumous success of Owen's work and it was rare for Osbert to celebrate other poets. His priority then became bringing together all Owen's manuscripts and publishing a collected edition of his work. "It must be a success – and I think it would be a good thing to write a short preface."

He wrote to Mrs Owen to urge her on: "Wilfred's poems ought to be seen about at once. I am sure I could get them taken by Blackwell at Oxford ... but I advise a London publisher – and would act for you in this matter or get Siegfried to do so. So will you command me about this?"

BLOOMSBURY POETS

Other, less tragic, poetic stars were in the making, and in December the previous year, 1917, the Sitwells met the rising Eliot at a charity poetry reading at the literary patrons and reviewers, Lady Colefax and Sir Edmund Gosse's. It was held in a wealthy terrace of Regent's Park, South Kensington and the other readers included Irene Rutherford McLeod who read poems by Sassoon. Eliot had been kept late at Lloyds Bank (where he worked) and so arrived late in checked trousers. He was rebuked by Gosse but Edith was taken with him and found him slim and elegant although a little pale. Osbert said he was reserved and armoured with fine manners, though always lively and jaunty – similar to the quality of his poetry.

Eliot and his neurotic wife Vivien subsequently attended Edith's Saturday afternoon tea parties, which she called "bun" parties, at 22 Pembridge Mansions, and would also have tea with the Sitwells in a café near Marble Arch, regularly arriving later than everyone else. Yet whilst the Sitwell's admired Eliot his work was not in *Wheels*. It was an anthology that Eliot complained contained too many "garden-gods, guitars and mandolins." And in a letter to Pound he called the Sitwells the Shitwells.

As these literary stars were ascending others were fading. George Moore, a thin, elderly Irishman with a side parting and waxed moustache belonged to an older school of writers. He wore a starched collar under which was a lively spirit, that showed through his bright eyes. On one occasion, in 1918, at the house of Sir Edmund and Lady Gosse, Edith Sitwell was with Moore.

She wrote; "Mr Moore had not, I think, arrived in a very happy frame of mind; and this state was aggravated by the conversational habits of another guest. At first Mr. Moore remained steeped in an impenetrable gloom, but after a while he turned to me, and in a voice shaking with indignation, hissed: "Yes, yes, yes, forty million thousand yes's. How can I talk when someone says yes, yes, yes?" To this question, no answer could be returned, so I remained silent. Afterwards Mr. Moore relented so far as to speak of a most interesting book called the Bible, which contained the intimate history of a most interesting people, the Jews, and, as well, to inform me that he had discovered there was a vehicle called an omnibus which would take one to any destination, should one be fortunate enough to attract its attention. As we left the house Mr. Moore perceived one of these vehicles, and rushed toward it crying "Omnibus, Omnibus!" But alas, he was not fortunate on this occasion, and did not attract the attention of the omnibus, which went on its way without him."

Moore was the literary rival of Thomas Hardy. Hardy's novels sustained Sassoon through the war, however, even the traditional Sassoon was not enthusiastic about Moore's work. In 1917 Sassoon read Moore's novel about Christ *The Brook Kerith* and found it beautiful. Then in 1918 he tried some more Moore and found it unpleasant so went back to Hardy whom he idolised.

Hardy had a wizened face, a bald crown with grey hair brushed back at the sides, bushy eyebrows and a long grey waxed moustache. He dressed as a country gentleman and looked like a retired general, wearing a thick, three-piece tweed suit with white shirt and black tie. Sassoon would visit Hardy who thought that Sassoon should keep the title of Captain even though the war had ended. And Sassoon collected together, and presented to Hardy, a collection of poems by various young poets to mark Hardy's 79th birthday in 1919.

Whilst not exactly Georgians Hardy and Moore represented an older style of work. The Sitwells and Eliot were developing work in new directions away from them and another key group, the Bloomsbury Group, were developing it in yet another direction.

The leading light of this movement was Virginia Woolf, a dark haired and thin lady with large eyes and a sallow face. She was ethereal as if aware of subtler forces. And along with her husband, Leonard, they had set up the Hogarth Press in 1917.

In 1918 Eliot met Virginia and whilst the Bloomsbury group were not then famous Eliot found them interesting in their sexual and social candour, though he kept a distance from the other writers in the Group. It was a connection that was treated with suspicion by his wife Vivien and mocked by Pound.

AFTER THE WAR

Eliot continued to drink in London teashops with Osbert and Sacheverell. They ate in restaurants in Piccadilly and lunched in Eliot's flat. Osbert sent Eliot a brace of pheasants in 1919 though Eliot never really admitted to the help and social status that they gave him. When the number of subscribers to Osbert's *Art and Letters* failed to grow Osbert detected a conspiracy to oust him in favour of Eliot. Osbert wrote to Eliot who was perplexed and cross at the idea. Then Osbert saw the rumours as a plot to create a split between him and Eliot. However, Eliot had by now become cross with Osbert as he felt that Osbert had copied his quatrain style and became better know for it. And Eliot was at pains to emphasise that he had done it first.

The threat to Eliot was real as Osbert's work and status was greater than his own at that time. In 1919 a luncheon was given in Osbert's honour at the Savoy Hotel to send him on his way to New York to promote his first novel. Sixty guests turned up and paid for the luncheon including Sassoon, Arnold Bennett, Clive Bell, the cartoonist David Low, William Walton, H.G. Wells and Humbert Wolfe. In New York his distinguished American publisher, George Doran, gave a large dinner in his honour and whilst Sassoon had tried to organise a lecture tour around the country for Osbert he never left New York.

Sassoon actively promoted his friends, and in 1919 he nominated Edith to become the first Georgian poet. She didn't appreciate this as she had set up *Wheels* in opposition to the Georgians. Sassoon felt at home with neither intellectuals nor the working classes. But Sassoon liked Edith's work and wanted poetry that was close to the non-intellectual Georgian style of speaking the simple language of the heart, in "direct utterance."

Edith liked his war poems as they were anti-establishment in content rather than technique. Her highest praise came much later, in 1928, and was for *The Heart's Journey.* She wrote "Poetry doesn't come by bellowing to attract the attention of the crowd. It is much more like taming a wild bird in a wood – one has to do it in silence. You have tamed the wild bird and no mistake." It was based on instinct and intellect but for Edith it was still too traditional in technique. Like Pound she preferred the use of symbols as in Imagism and an internal music to a poem rather than a strict verse. However this new form was already criticised by the new poet, Robert Graves whose poems had been included in Georgian Poetry anthologies, a form he also, ironically, described as a "dead movement contemporary with Imagism".

THE "ZULU" ARRIVES

Meanwhile, younger poets were beginning to join the new movements. In 1919 Roy Campbell, a 6'2" slim, broad shouldered and graceful South Africa went to study in Oxford. Before going up to Oxford he had allied himself to Edith's *Wheels*. His face was strong but sensitive, with a thin-lipped mouth curled in witty amusement. His large eyes were blue green and slanted like a cats. They grew pale when angry and full of colour when enthused by conversation or in sharing his encyclopaedic knowledge of literature, history and painting. His hair was receding at the temples so he appeared older and wiser. And he was shy in groups until loosened up with alcohol.

In 1919 Campbell had a homosexual affair with a young composer William Walton. Walton introduced him to Wyndham

Lewis and also took him to one of Edith's "bun" parties at 22 Pembridge Mansions. The parties were frequent and there Campbell and Sassoon stood tall, "soaring above the smoke and babel like an innocent pink crane." There Campbell met Osbert, Sacheverell and Eliot. He took up the Sitwell cause amongst the undergraduates at Oxford, seeing *Wheels* "as a very necessary but badly written hypothesis on which to work our theorems". And he championed the new poetry of Eliot and the new prose of Lewis.

Campbell wrote to his father from Oxford; "Art is not developed by a lot of long-haired fools in velvet jackets. It develops itself and pulls these fools wherever it wants them to go. It reacts more thoroughly and easily than the most sensitive artist in the world... The Georgians, those who in the reign of George V (in the age of machinery, and probably one of the most important stages in the history of our evolution) persist in groping amongst the dust of ancient folios for what they write. They are treading the same ground that was trodden by the Elizabethans 400 years ago – and they are not treading it half so well what is their importance? If a man wants to read that style of work he will surely read Ben Jonson or Marlowe. So it is pretty certain that our Georgian friends will fizzle out pretty soon."

However, in 1920 Campbell had to leave Oxford due to lack of progress in learning Ancient Greek. He left for London and became known as "The Zulu", a name coined for him by Lewis. As well as making a name for himself as a writer Campbell was also becoming known as a volatile person. He had a fight with sculptor Jacob Epstein in Campbell's flat, whilst diners ate below in The Harlequin Restaurant, because Epstein had accused him of having an affair with his sisters.

And these artistic personalities often had an inability to connect. This could be seen on Thursday evenings in 1920. When Osbert dined with Sacheverell and several other writers including Lewis and Pound in a restaurant in Piccadilly Circus. Lewis wrote how each writer sat at a separate table, the "distance helping to make conversation self-conscious or desultory. Pound was inclined to mumble into his red beard, a habit perhaps brought on by his defensiveness, the result in turn, of attacks delivered on himself during the years of his domicile in England. He was particularly a type the English do not understand or appreciate."

Criticism of each other was rife, though most frequently coming from Lewis; "But back to Osbert now. Osbert was once a minor Maecenas. He had *le bel air*, so much prized by the Baroness Bernstein-a Hanoverian hauteur and a beautiful lisp-which helped him out as a *raconteur*, and he was one of Chelsea's best. He threw quite a good dinner-party, in his salad days, and he was about the last person in London to mix 'mind' with his Mayfair. He would have been a 'baronet with a butterfly', under happier circumstances."

The conflicts were not helped by the presence of literary critics. At a dinner-party of January 22, 1920, Arnold Bennett, an influential critic for the *Evening Standard*, turned against Lewis. And Lewis, who was quick to attack others, was "touched on the raw" at even mild criticism.

Lewis said that; "Not long after the War I was at Osbert Sitwell's house for dinner (in Carlyle Square, Chelsea, it was) and Arnold Bennett and Walter Sickert were present .... At this dinner-party Sickert began talking about *"Tarr"*. I could see Bennett didn't like it. I think Sickert saw that too, for he went on talking about it more and more, at every moment in more ecstatic terms .... I saw that Bennett was extremely annoyed .... *Tarr* had been made to stink in his nostrils.... I knew that Sickert had made me an enemy though he had not meant to, for he is the kindest man in the world. For a number of years Arnold Bennett was a kind of book-dictator... The book-trade said that he could make a book overnight... The "author of *Tarr*" under this Dictatorship spent his time in a spiritual concentration camp-of barbed silence."

"As Sickert and I left the Sitwells that night (in 1922 or 3) I reproached him for having been so vehement with Bennett. But Sickert exclaimed against my retrospective objection. 'Nonsense! Why shouldn't he hear it! Of course he should be told- that and a lot more! *Quel comedie*-that such people as Arnold Bennett should be in a position of that sort-it is only in an age like ours that they could be! That one should have to talk to such people about *books* at all! Why should one be asked to meet such people? It is absurd that a Bennett should be referred to, for anything except the time of a train or the cost of a bicycle lamp! Pfui!"

Osbert, however, said that Sickert's had not praised *Tarr* and had attacked Lewis' paintings: "Sickert then lit a cigar and, nipping round the corner of the table, pressed one upon Lewis, with the words, "I give you this cigar because I so greatly admire your writings." Lewis switched upon him as dazzling a smile as he had had time to prepare-with him, everything was weighed and pre- meditated-but ... Sickert planted the goad by adding, "If I liked your paintings, I'd give you a bigger one!" ... Lewis, at this, became very angry, though typically, not with Sickert, but with the rest of the company. He refused, as a punishment, to accompany us to a party at Lady Ottoline Morrell's."

This was backed up by Arnold Bennett who said how Lewis was "there-in grey flannel. He left early-piqued, as some said, by remarks of Sickert."

Ch 4 : SASSOON "CUTS" OSBERT (1922)

Like many who fought in the war a return to convention was hard, even for the traditionalists like Sassoon. Walking through the London Club, with its hushed atmosphere, and its elderly gentlemen reclining in armchairs reading *The Times* and *Punch*. Sassoon felt most comfortable in a sort of master-apprentice relationship. He was intensely proud of his prestige as a 'man of letters' and that Hardy and the rest of them had accepted him as one of their clan. Yet here, in the club, he wanted to pick up a library stool, and throw it in a rugby pass to wake them up a bit.

Outside the club he walked across the London streets with total disregard of the traffic. He had been called "Mad Jack", for his action against the German guns in France and on Oxford Street car horns blared against him as tires squealed and drivers shouted protests.

He got to his Hunter Snipe 80 Drophead Coupe. He readily admitted that his driving was extreme; "My methods of turning from side roads into main roads were abrupt ..." He didn't signal and if there was an accident it was the other driver's fault.

Sassoon's friendship with Osbert deepened after staying for ten days with the brothers when he was in agony from sciatica. They had "behaved like angelic and agitated turtle doves. Almost always in a hurry, one or other seemed continually to be dashing up the steep stairs to look in and ask "How are you?"" However, Sassoon was more sensitive and shy than the Sitwells and began to feel overwhelmed by Osbert.

The relationship worsened when, in 1921 Sassoon spent a few days in Renishaw, the Sitwell family mansion and gardens, in Derbyshire. It was hard to reach, down wooded roads past coal mines and industrial villages. The house was set in a park, with a lake black with coal dust, and was a castellated mansion in discoloured Derbyshire stone. Inside it was a very dark hall and without electricity so they had to write by the light of oil lamps. The beautiful rooms were eclectically decorated with fine tapestry and paintings. Italian furniture sat under oak beams and plaster ceilings.

Sassoon became annoyed that the Sitwells would interrupt anyone who tried to have a serious conversation. And that Osbert wouldn't discuss anything for more than 2 minutes, wondering what time meals were and diverting his attention in many directions. This was a common complaint for visitors, who none-the-less enjoyed themselves.

Sassoon also complained that Osbert would keep discussing problems about money. He felt that Osbert worshipped his ancestors through their oil paintings and behaved like a Royal, either Hanoverian or like Louis XIV, yet was resentful of others' successes. To add to their difficulties Sassoon liked the Georgian poets and Osbert didn't. Sassoon also believed that whilst "Artists have a tendency towards vanity but I think that the greatest writers are almost invariably the most modest."

He wrote "All this Sitwell spite and trivial charade-satire makes me tired." "What a brilliant, disintegrating family they are!" "an absolute climax! Regency relics," their trouble is "too much taste."

Osbert wrote to Sassoon, "You are a difficult friend. If one goes to see you, you become tired, and feel that your blood is being sucked, I believe – and if one doesn't go to see you, where are you to be found?"

Behind it all there was a lurking sexual element in their relationship. This paralleled the sense of tension in the apparently harassed servants and gardeners who skulked around the grounds. In contrast, when Sassoon played croquet he would slam his opponent's balls away to the farthest flower-bed. And it was easy to see how Sassoon had been decorated for his reckless bravery and why he didn't enjoy social chatter.

There was also crazy behaviour late at night and the house was haunted with a ghost who apparently did nothing more than utter a meaningful hiss.

Sassoon grew weary and noted, with despondency, that whilst there was a large and ornamental lake it was "too shallow for an effective suicide."

Their relationship reached its lowest point after the *London Mercury* published some of Graves' writings and the Sitwells resented Graves' success in comparison to Osbert's. Osbert, under the pseudonym "Augustine Rivers", published *The Death of Mercury* in the final edition of *Wheels*, 1921 in which he satirized Graves and others.

Sassoon knew that Graves hoped to earn his living as a poet and support his family in that way. His lack of success was leading to a loss of self- confidence and causing problems in his marriage. Sassoon noted in his diary - "How petty they are with their endless family lampoons on the *"London Mercury.""* "As long as they go on like that they can hardly expect to be taken seriously ... I have the advantage of being more successful as a writer. I have no cause to be jealous of Graves and Blunden, etc., as Osbert has always been."

And so in November 1921 Sassoon followed Osbert out of a concert at Wigmore Hall and deliberately "cut" him on the pavement to hurt his feelings. Despite "cutting" him Sassoon was obsessed with their relationship and wrote, "I suddenly realised that my attitude towards O is strongly sadistic,... I saw, quite calmly, that my (supposed) stab at his feelings this afternoon aroused in me acute sexual feelings towards him. (I'd never before been conscious of any sexual feelings toward him except a slight repugnance.)" He felt that his unexpected reaction arose because Osbert was "such a vivid (though unsympathetic) character. I can't hope to blot him out of my life and thoughts."

A wounded Osbert told Sassoon, "You have a streak in your character that makes you derive a little pleasure, as well as much pain from humiliating your friends."

Then in June 1922 Osbert made conciliatory gestures which Sassoon was tempted to accept but vehemently rejected. Sassoon wrote that "I intend to keep him at more than arm's length for several more months,"... "He is a case where one must assert one's independence." "Something in his character makes it impossible for me to feel kindly towards him. His neurotic spite and jealousy are ill-concealed by his 'social charm'. He seems incapable of serenity, or of tolerance of his contemporaries. His portrait should be a restless reflection in a valuable gilt Chippendale mirror. Peacock *en casserole* should be his staple diet. How tiresome he can be with his everlasting chatter about his antiquarian father; and his disreputably aristocratic mama; and his untidy financial affairs. Perhaps I am severe on him, but he is always merciless to everyone but himself and his brother and sister."

Then that summer they met, by chance, in Venice. Sassoon looked through him: "It is the arrogance of the artist. Until I have humiliated or dominated him I will not be satisfied." But Osbert was not aware that either was required of him. And so it was only with time that the feud died down. They met unexpectedly again, this time in Pall Mall, London. Neither smiled but both "forgot to scowl". After this they sent each other humorously offensive postcards and Sassoon sent Osbert a long letter describing everything that he considered to be wrong in Osbert's character.

During this period, however, Sassoon still admired Edith's work as original, beautiful and having fantastic plumage. And so they went together to dinner parties where they supported each other. And she requested of him that if one of her more vicious literary rivals "drags me to a secluded corner, Siegfried, I shall be obliged if you will kindly come too, otherwise I shall be torn to bits."

Edith frequently invited Sassoon to tea and offered to teach him how to cook chops, worried that he wasn't eating enough. She requested that he "please turn over a new leaf about it. Neglect of meals leads to a breakdown sooner or later."

Sassoon affectionately called her "stormy spinster petrel" and Sacheverell believed that Edith was in love with Sassoon, though was probably not interested in a sexual relationship. There friendship was so strong that when Sassoon once made criticism of her poetry Edith warned "my word, if it had been

anyone but you who had told me to "consider and reconsider",
and "sift" my poems, I should have taken that person on a one-
way journey. Luckily, it was you. – But the escape has been
narrow."

However, by 1924 even they had fallen-out. Edith told
Arnold Bennett how Siegfried Sassoon wouldn't speak to Osbert
now because Osbert would never leave him alone. He wouldn't
speak to her, because she wouldn't stop Osbert doing his tricks.
These "tricks" included when Siegfried "cut me dead at a party,
- because Osbert had mistaken an enlarged photograph of
W.J.Turner for a map of Vesuvius."

"But what can I do," said Edith to Arnold Bennett. Adding
that in revenge Sacheverell swore he would never speak to
Siegfried again. And also that it appeared that either Siegfried
wouldn't speak to Robert Graves or vice versa.

So Arnold Bennett arranged a reconciliation between
Osbert and Sassoon over lunch at the Reform Club. Sassoon
drew back but Bennett made him come. And he also made
Sassoon escort Osbert from the club. The next time they met in
the street they chatted amicably and Osbert gave Sassoon a toy
fish in a small glass globe. They did not become close friends
again, but Sassoon stopped attacking Osbert in his diary and
asked himself "Are the Sitwells worth worrying about?"

Despite his reservations the Sitwells, for the post-war
generation, were a refreshing inspiration. Edith had genius and
Osbert and Sacheverell had panache. They were in the
establishment and yet against it, serious yet light hearted, hard
working yet hedonists.

And when Sassoon reconciled with Osbert in 1924 he
reconciled with Edith by default. However, he kept his distance
and Sassoon told Osbert "I like reading people's books. But I
find that knowing literary people personally leads to disaster. I
like to be aloof – to watch people."

Osbert believed Sassoon's dislike of Modernism gave rise
to his hostility to the Bloomsbury Group and stunted his growth
as a poet. However, by 1922 Sassoon felt that he needed to
spend time catching up with the intellectualism of literary

figures such as the Bloomsbury Group, but wrote "whether their brains are worth catching up, I don't yet know."

Sassoon became friends with members of the Group, and when invited to dine with Virginia in 1923 he had to explain to her "I am not at all intellectual – in fact I have a very cumbersome mind." He found the evening "a gossipy affair, very pleasant and unconstrained." Her husband, Leonard Woolf, was "reticent and rather weary but Virginia was 'charming', drawing him out adroitly to gossip about mutual friends and acquaintances." He was pleased that she thought that Eliot was "rather an old prig, really" and that he personified the sterility and artificiality of Modernism. She said that he needed to be "chaffed out of it" and was absurdly formal and prim. She found him "a nice dear kind sensitive warm-hearted fellow" and was not disturbed by his practicing homosexuality (which was then illegal). And she urged Sassoon to write for her own publishing company, Hogarth Press, which in 1923 was to publish Graves' *The Feather Bed.*

Sassoon's second meeting with Virginia in 1924 left her wishing for "More brain, O God, more brain!" Sassoon followed the Georgian line of thinking that authentic poetry came from genuine experience and that Modern verse was too cerebral and without heart. Sassoon's opinions were unlikely to please Virginia's. In his own words; "I do not to understand a great deal of modern poetry. I placed the blame for this upon myself rather than upon the writers. So many contemporary poets don't interest me. They stir no chords. They awake no imaginative response. Why then should I read them?"

Leaning back in his armchair, his long leg cocked over the arm, Sassoon considered that, "I see myself as a man who has a gift. It is none of my business how I got it, but it is there, and I and the rest of the world must recognize it." He struck his chest with his fist, "I am a poet of the heart. A ham poet. I can't write about anything else. I'm just ham!"

Ch 5 : THE PORTRAIT OF EDITH (1922)

In 1921 Siegfried Sassoon was one of many literary figures to be drawn by William Rothenstein. However, Rothenstein had come to be seen as a traditional artist and not the only artist of choice in our world of poets.

Wyndham Lewis was creating a new pathway in both literary and artistic worlds. Before the war he had founded the Vorticist painters movement, published his novel *Tarr* and the Vorticist literary manifesto *BLAST*. Lewis saw active service as a bombardier during the war. And shortly after the war ended he had his first one-man show in London in 1919 with a style of work that had become less abstract. And his literary and artistic lives were to combine in his drawings and paintings of Edith Sitwell.

Lewis met Edith in 1921 and his relationship with her was more difficult than with her brothers. She was six feet tall, pale-faced and lank-haired, with a curvature of the spine and a long curved nose. However, both had the original genius of an outsider.

Edith said how; "Mr. Lewis spent a very large part of time with my brothers and me in the years 1921, 22, 23 and this was a great delight to us for we have always considered him as the greatest prose writer of our generation and as a great draughtsman." He paid their family a visit at one of their houses, in Scarborough, "arriving with a very dark complexion and a bundle in place of a suitcase. My mother, I am afraid, did not take a fancy to him and asked Osbert: "Has your friend brought a valet?" she was promptly escorted to bed and asked to remain there. The visit I believe passed off without any other incident, but I do not know for I was not there."

The Sitwells' mother, Lady Ida, had a dual character. Osbert Sitwell saw her as "Now a person of the utmost distinction and beauty, ... she belonged to an earlier, less hackneyed age, in which the standards of Woolworth mass production did not exist." However, he said that she had "cruelly ill-used" Edith, yet when Edith became famous Lady Ida "had come to love her society, her wit and perception, and it was symptomatic of Edith's fineness of character that she responded."

At Renishaw, the Sitwell family home in Derbyshire, Sir George Sitwell would appear for meals in white tie and tail coat. He and Lady Ida never appeared together at meals. He was very gentle and was a garden designer with an interest in the Middle Ages. He disapproved of alcohol and people sitting to dinner would be lucky to get more than one glass of wine."

Nor was there any port or brandy after dinner. Lady Ida would secretly bid some of the guests to her upstairs sitting room before dinner for discreet drinks. Lady Ida needed attention and typically the footman would assemble the family to hear a message that her ladyship wanted to see Miss Edith upstairs. "I can't go. I've been with her all day. Osbert, you go." "Sachie, you go." Eventually the Footman would say "Well, come on. One of you's got to go."

Lewis also visited them at Renishaw and Edith wrote that "...this visit, alas, was not entirely happy, for he mislaid his collar on the morning after his arrival, and could not come down to luncheon until he had found it. But eventually Robins, Osbert's delightful ex-soldier servant (by this time butler at Renishaw), tracked it down, and it flapped back on to Lewis's neck, much as a weary and rather dilapidated blackbird might return to its nest." Edith noted, "There are men who seem to have been born without relations but with a collar, and Lewis was one of these. He remained immured in this faithful friend and I think it must have figured on his passport. Certainly one had only to add up the rings on it (made by time) as one adds up the rings on a palm tree or on the horns of an antelope, to arrive at some estimate of his age."

Edith continued, "At this time however, we were counted among his friends and Sacheverell and I were inured to the ordeal of Mr. Lewis watching us from afar with that blinking look of reproachful affection to which I have referred; a look which turned upon us, varied from the expression of the canine friend in the well-known advertisement of his master's voice, to that of a returning wanderer seeing from afar the old homestead."

PORTRAIT

Edith went to be painted by Lewis in his Adam and Eve studio in 1923, wearing a short fur coat and outlandish hat. She was jeered at by children in the street, so pulled a face and stuck out her tongue. It silenced them. And Lewis' appearance was no less striking.

Edith said how "His studio was situated in a piece of waste ground, off Kensington High Street, and haunted by pallid hens, squawking desolately and prophetically; and the appearance of Mr.Lewis's hair aroused in some observers the conviction that the feathers of these had sought within its shades a refuge from the general confusion. Another school of thought, however, ascribed the alien substances by which it seemed to be bestrewn to a different cause, believing them to be a sprinkling of the snows of time. For the nature of his toilette, and his general appearance, undoubtedly aroused attention and gave rise to speculation."

"His complexion always dark, was at moments darker than others; and this pigmentation was due to no freak of Nature or chance, but to habits and choice. His clothes seemed as much a refuge as a covering, and when fully equipped to face the world and the weather, he presented much the same appearance as that which we are privileged to see in photographs of certain brave men at the very moment of their rescue after six months spent among the Polar wastes and the blubber."

Lewis also seemed to ramble inanely. One afternoon Edith arrived for a sitting to find him shaving.

"D'you mind waiting whilst I shave?"

"Not at all."

Lewis heaved a sigh. "And *after* I've shaved, I mean to *wash my hands*." He sighed again. "I suppose you do everything one after another, don't you? I mean you probably have a bath in the morning?"

Edith assented.

"And after that, you probably brush your hair?"

Edith agreed. Lewis remembered something and retraced his steps with great despondency. "But *before* that you - brush your teeth?"

"Yes."

Mr. Lewis gave an even deeper sigh. "It's that damned *Time*! I seem to have so little Time for anything. Now sometimes I'll wash my hands in the morning – and shave in the afternoon. At other times I'll..." he reflected. "Well, I suppose I'd better get on with what I'm doing."

Edith said that he always pretended that he was being watched or noticed, behaving so oddly that he "attracted immediately that attention which might not, otherwise, have been forthcoming."

"His outward personality, his shield against the world, changed from day to day – one might almost say from hour to hour. When he grinned, one felt as if one were looking at a lantern slide ... a click, a fade-out, and another slide, totally unconnected with it, and equally unreal, had taken its place. He was no longer the simple-minded artist, but a rather sinister, piratic, formidable Dago. For this remarkable man had a habit of appearing in various roles, partly as a disguise (for caution was part of his professional equipment) and partly in order to defy his own loneliness.

For in this way so many different characters inhabited his studio (all enclosed in his own body, so that they had no opportunity of contradicting him or paying him insufficient attention and homage) that he had scarcely any need of outside companionship. He had to appear in different roles in order to impress himself and if possible, others."

And one of his favourite roles was a Spanish one, "in which he would assume a gay, if sinister, manner, very masculine and gallant, and deeply impressive to a feminine observer. He would wear a sombrero and allow the expression "Caramba!" to escape him..."

He wore a black patch, which he changed from eye to eye according to who was sitting next to him. When both eyes were uncovered, "they wore a blinking look of yearning and reproachful affection, extremely disconcerting to the object of the gaze."

"His life was overshadowed by real, or imaginary, dangers. He was, for instance, a prey to the conviction that Roger Fry (*an influential artist and contemporary of William Rothenstein*) roosted, permanently, on the roof of his studio, in order to observe his slightest movement. Then too, there either were (or were not) the rats. At one time Mr. Lewis got it into his head that these were lurking amidst the confusion.

"D'you mind rats?" he enquired.

Edith replied "I do."

"Well, they're here all right. Night and day. Day and night. But I'll try to keep them off." With which he gave a swish to his brush and went on painting."

There were definitely mice, which steadily grew bolder, resting against the furniture and staring insolently. They even climbed upon one poet's knee and stared disapprovingly at his face. So Lewis bought a large gong to bang at the opening of the mouse-hole to force them to retreat.

And objects would fly past Edith as she sat for her portrait as "...Mr. Lewis would give a savage kick to the varying and warring objects which hid the floor from view and which seemed to spend their whole time clamouring for his attention, so that he frequently presented the appearance of a harassed mother returning home with her wearied and quarrelsome offspring after a particularly noisy Bank Holiday."

Edith sat for him every day but Sunday for ten months. Then the sittings ended abruptly in 1923. Many drawings were completed but the major portrait was unfinished and left with no hands, a feature of which she was especially proud.

Edith claimed that Lewis professed his love and then she ceased to sit. Edith remained a virgin through life and there is no indication that she was love with him. Edith told friends that Lewis "was, unfortunately, seized with a kind of schwiirmerei for me. I did not respond. It did not go very far, but was a nuisance as he would follow me about, staring in a most trying manner and telling our acquaintances about the schwiirmerei. So, eventually, I stopped sitting to him."

In protest against this explanation Lewis said of Edith, that "Except for her hands, she insisted that she had no beauty. She disliked the word 'plain'; she thought of herself as ugly." He said that Edith "tells her public that 'once she was a golden woman.' Nothing answering to that description was ever visible to me, I may say, at the time to which I suppose she refers. She had practically no hair, and such as she possessed was anything but 'golden': it was a dirty lemon. She was so round-shouldered that it almost amounted to a hump. She was hollow chested, with a long frozen nose, down which she looked and sneered to show her father was a baronet."

Lewis' may have found her attractive or was just following his impulse to sleep with every woman who sat for him. The truth can't be known.

Edith was adamant about the cause. She wrote that "it would be ridiculous to deny that Mr. Lewis was a very considerable writer. If he were not so completely jaundiced that all colours, good and evil, seemed to him as one he would, indeed, have been a great one." However, she added that "Lewis enjoyed lying, not only as a defence behind which he could hide, but as an idol. It may be said that when he himself called Cato's truth, or the expedient lie, was his god."

"When Lewis is dead I shall write the story of his life…and in it I shall show how every little fault and every little mistake made by this fundamentally gentle and affectionate character is the result of the fear that engrosses him, the fear that he is not loved, the crushing impressions that those on whom he has set his affections do not return them."

Edith pointed out that he had many such conflicts. "It is sad to think how many friends changed into enemies (in Mr. Lewis's imagination) for no reason. He was very angry for instance with Frank Dobson, the sculptor, (*who sculpted the brass busts of both Osbert*) for claiming that Mr. Lewis was older than himself. "I am thirty-four" he informed Sacheverell in a furious voice "and I remain 34 until further notice." We all thought at the time that Mr. Lewis was rather minimising the fact. But he liked the facts about himself to remain shrouded in mystery, ... He is a great writer and a most sad and solitary man having attacked and driven away every loyal friend he possessed, and all those whose admiration for his gifts is founded in reality."

In the 1930s Lewis repainted and completed the portrait without her. In it she wears a helmet-like hat over an angular face, nose and lips. She sits in green and gold clothing, and has metal tube-like hands. All of this gives her an inhuman, mechanical character. This is reinforced by the shelf of Lewis' books, the angular door, the chair and the blue columns that balance the work. This painting shows that despite disagreements he admired her contributions to art and poetry. And he showed her in an impressive manner and in an excellent example of his style

Ch 6 : *ULYSSES* AND *THE WASTELAND* (1923)

In 1917 T.S. Eliot, who did not serve in the war, began to attract attention not so much for his poetry as his behaviour. He wore thick greenish powder on his face and spoke in a pedantic yet slightly drunken voice. Ezra Pound advised him to drop this role of "wild man" and instead to play a polite and precise young man. Pound pointed out that "there was no use of two of us butting a stone wall; that he would never be as hefty a battering ram as I was, nor as explosive as Lewis, and that he had better try a more oceanic and fluid method of sapping the foundations." So Eliot adopted a bowler hat, a double breasted sit and carried a tightly rolled up umbrella. He became the English Gentleman who would eventually kill the poetry of the English Gentleman.

In 1918 Eliot, like the Bloomsbury Group, attacked Georgian poetry as "inbred" and "insipid". Eliot was accepted by the Group and associated with Virginia and Leonard Woolf because he was a Modernist who wanted to break down traditional form and fracture language.

In the 1920s Eliot dined and stayed with them several times. Initially they found him to be extremely formal and on 19th September 1920, Virginia (the leading novelist of the Bloomsbury Group) noted "The odd thing about Eliot, is that his eyes are lively and youthful when the cast of his face and the shape of his sentences are formal and even heavy."

Leonard noted "He was so inhibited, those sentences were so formal and heavy that, although - or rather because - I had seen so much in his poetry and in those eyes which seemed to escape from him, the week-end left me with a feeling of disappointment. In conversation it was his brain that was disappointing, so much more rigid and less powerful than I had expected from the poems, and with so little play of mind."

However, Leonard said "he was easy and unreticent - and always very interesting" about literature. Virginia and Leonard believed that they loosened "up the pomposity and priggishness which constricted him, with thawing out the essential warmth of his nature which, when we first knew him, seemed to be enclosed in an envelope of frozen formality."

Leonard broke the ice. Eliot "was walking with Virginia and me across the fields down to the river. I suddenly wanted to make water and fell behind to do so. Neither of my companions saw what I was doing, but I suppose it was very obvious what I was doing. Anyhow, when I caught them up again, I felt that Tom was uncomfortable, even shocked. I asked him whether he was and he said yes, and we then had what gradually became a perfectly frank conversation about conventions and formality. Tom said that he not only could not possibly have done what I did, that he would never dream of shaving in the presence even of his wife."

And by 1920 Virginia wrote of the insecurities that she had expressed to Eliot, "Eliot coming on the heel of a long stretch of writing fiction made me listless; cast shade upon me; and the mind when engaged upon fiction wants all its boldness and self-confidence. He said nothing – but I reflected how what I'm doing is probably being better done by Mr Joyce." She was also worried about not being as good as more established poets, like Keats. To which Eliot replied "Yes, we are. We're trying something harder."

Leonard wrote how in March 1921 Virginia still called Eliot Eliot and wondered "whether we would ever get to the stage of Christian names: 'But what about Eliot? Will he become Tom? What happens with friendships undertaken at the age of 40? Do they flourish and live long? I suppose a good mind endures, and one is drawn to it and sticks to it, owing to having a good mind myself. Not that Tom endures my writing, damn him.' By the end of the year we were calling him Tom and Virginia noted with regret that she was no longer frightened of him."

BLOOMSBURY AGAINST JOYCE

Eliot was a real challenge to the Bloomsburies status as chief cultural innovators, as were Pound's other protégés Lewis and James Joyce. They were his literary machines and his ambition, was; "To break the pentometer, that was the first heave."

The novelist James Joyce was a tall and assured Irishman. His raised hair was brushed back but still wild. And his round glasses, bow-tie and goatee beard gave him the look of a professor researching into the worlds of excess.

When Pound received a copy of the initial sections of Joyce's *Ulysses* in 1917 he called Joyce's descriptions of sexual and excremental functions as arsthetic. And he thought that it was the most astonishing Modernist text since Eliot's *Prufrock*.

Ulysses took longer to write than expected. The sexually explicit and hallucinatory episode in which Leopold Bloom visits a brothel at midnight was not completed until January 1921. And Joyce eventually finished the book in Paris in October 1921. He had intended to spend a week in the city when he arrived on 8th July 1920, but he and his wife Nora stayed twenty years. They arrived broke but Ezra Pound found them free lodgings in a flat owned by a friend. Pound then introduced Joyce to the city's cultural community. He met an American, Sylvia Beach, who owned a small bookshop in Paris and she was a supporter of Joyce's work.

The long and difficult novel was a stream-of-consciousness modernist extravaganza. Joyce parodied past and present literary styles, beginning with Homer and ending with Joyce. He portrayed the same scene in romantic, scientific, journalistic and historic prose styles, in an endless process with no truth to be found, just a world of 'appearances'.

Joyce also had a patron, Harriet Shaw Weaver, who supported his complex world. Virginia recalled that "I remember Miss Weaver, in wool gloves, bringing Ulysses in typescript to our tea table at Hogarth House. Roger I think sent her. Would we devote our lives to printing it? The indecent pages looked so incongruous: she was spinsterly, buttoned up. And the pages reeled with indecency. I put it in the drawer of the inlaid cabinet." And even though scandalous sex was common to the conversation of the Bloomsburies Virginia refused to publish *Ulysses*. But in February 1922 it was published by Shakespeare and Company.

It was published in Paris and copies had to be smuggled into Britain and America. 499 copies were seized by Customs at Folkestone and 500 copies were seized and burned in New York.

Many of the reviews were unfavourable, partly because Joyce had been critical of fellow Irish writers and George Moore's response was that it was "hopeless" and that "Joyce thinks because he prints all the dirty little words he is a great novelist."

However, Pound praised Joyce for his "epoch-making report on the state of the human mind in the twentieth century." And Eliot called him "The greatest master of the English language since Milton".

In August 1922 Virginia wrote "I should be reading *Ulysses*, and fabricating my case for and against. I have read 200 pages so far - not a third; and have been amused, stimulated, charmed, interested, by the first 2 or 3 chapters - to the end of the cemetery scene; and then puzzled, bored, irritated and disillusioned by a queasy undergraduate scratching his pimples. And Tom, great Tom, thinks this on a par with War and Peace! An illiterate, underbred book it seems to me; the book of a self taught working man, and we all know how distressing they are, how egotistic, insistent, raw, striking, and ultimately nauseating. When one can have the cooked flesh, why have the raw? But I think if you are anaemic, as Tom is, there is a glory in blood. Being fairly normal myself I am soon ready for the classics again. I may revise this later. I do not compromise my critical sagacity. I plant a stick in the ground to mark page 200."

In September 1922 she wrote again; "There was a good deal of talk about Ulysses. Tom said, "He is a purely literary writer. He is founded upon Walter Pater with a dash of Newman." I said he was virile - a he-goat; but didn't expect Tom to agree. Tom did though; and said he left out many things that were important. The book would be a landmark, because it destroyed the whole of the 19th Century. It left Joyce himself with nothing to write another book on. It showed up the futility of all the English styles. He thought some of the writing beautiful. But there was no "great conception"; that was not Joyce's intention. He thought that Joyce did completely what he meant to do."

THE WASTELAND

Eliot was greatly influenced by Joyce. In 1920 he and Lewis had visited Joyce, bringing a parcel of a pair of old brown shoes from Pound. They found him pleasant but arrogant and dismissive of his literary contemporaries. They expected Joyce to be hard-up but Harriet Weaver had given him £2,000 and Joyce took them to dinner and then gave the waiter a huge tip.

The next day Lewis and Eliot went cycling. Lewis was speeding on his hired bicycle when its handlebars snapped off. He was thrown violently off and landed on the road, badly injuring his knee. He was furious and returned the bicycle to the proprietor who blamed Lewis for damaging his machine and wanted money in compensation. The two also visited a monastery and at the end of the day Eliot's different temperament was shown as he took out a small notebook to entered the days expenses as they drank armagnac in a café.

Eliot visited Paris again in the autumn of 1921 after spending the summer in a sanitorium in Lausanne. He had suffered a nervous breakdown through a combination of his own worries and of his wife's nervous complaints. This may have inspired him in writing his experimental poem *The Waste Land* and he wrote: "It is commonplace that some forms of illness are extremely favorable, not only to religious illumination, but to artistic and literary composition. A piece of writing meditated, apparently without progress for months or years, may suddenly take shape and word; and in this state long passages may be produced which require little or no retouch,"

Eliot brought Pound his first draft of *The Waste Land* which Pound saw as powerful as *Ulysses* but thought that it should be half the size. And so he began marking the manuscript with comments.

Eliot returned to his bank job in London and completed the poem with the cuts that Pound thought were needed for it to have impact. Eliot dedicated the poem to him as "il miglior fabbro," the greater craftsman, words that had been used to describe Dante. Pound, who struggled with writing his own *The Cantos*, returned the praise "Complimenti, you bitch. I am wracked by the seven jealousies, and cogitating an excuse for always exuding my deformative secretions in my own stuff, and never getting an outline."

Ulysses and *The Waste Land* inspired Pound to use myth as a narrative device to connect parts of a whole though he would eventually radically remove all traditional dramatic exposition from his work.

Pound was concerned that Eliot might have a more serious nervous breakdown after returning to work in the bank and to a home life with his emotionally disturbed wife. He wrote on how artists should be freed from drudgery so that they can focus on invention. "The only thing one can give an artist is leisure in which to work." And that the "worst waste in contemporary literature," was Eliot's bank employment. For Pound, Eliot was a prisoner who needed to be released from drudgery. Without an aristocracy or organized civilization left to select the best: "Only those of us who know what civilization is, only those of us who want better literature, not more literature, better art, not more art, can be expected to pay for it. No use waiting for the masses to develop a finer taste, they aren't moving that way,."

So he created a project called "Bel Esprit" which was a fund for patrons to contribute ten pounds to promote good writing "for life or as long as Eliot needs it." And thanks to this fund Eliot eventually left his work in Lloyd's Bank and then became a director of Faber & Gwyer, publishers in 1927, able to devote his time to literature.

In 1922 Eliot finished *The Waste Land* and published it in his own magazine the *Criterion*. The apparently meaningless montage of literary styles contained scholarly allusions to the history of literature, to poets like Dante and Milton, but broke up verse like the Great War had broken up European civilisation. He informed Virginia that in writing the final section of the stream-of-consciousness poem "I wasn't even bothering whether I understood what I was saying. I was in a trance. Retreated from worldly caress into that amorphous sea I had known as a child."

The Waste Land captured the mood of disillusionment and cynicism that characterised the post-war years for the artistic elite. It marked the end of Georgian ascendancy and Eliot became the messenger for his generation. Eliot became a leader (thought Lewis and Virginia wouldn't have seen him as such) and even Sassoon, who had a campaign against Modernism, called Eliot "Towering Tom".

Edith said that Eliot was "one of the greatest [poets] of the last one hundred and fifty years" who had "flooded himself with the immediate age as with vast oceanic tides". She said he was "a shy creature, always very carefully dressed. I do hate romantic wanderers who are too great spirits to be in the city. Tom Eliot was a bank clerk for ages and is still a publisher!" In 1922 Osbert noticed to Sacheverell, at a dinner party, the powder Eliot wore on his face was "pale but distinctly green, the colour of forced lily-of-the-valley." Osbert thought that it was to give him a look of suffering and to provoke sympathy. He was unlikely to have powdered his face before going to work at the bank so it may have been to make him look more a poet than a banker. Either way, it made him look chilling and aloof, characteristics suited to the writer of *The Waste Land*.

The Hogarth Press also printed *The Waste Land* in 1923 at which time Eliot's relationship with literary society was strained through his neurotic wife Vivienne. Edith and Virginia noticed an overwhelming smell of ether as Vivienne entered a room. She used this to rub over her body to alleviate headaches caused by a hormonal imbalance. Vivienne wanted Eliot to leave his job at the bank to become the literary editor of the *Nation* magazine – a position which the Sitwells and Virginia urged him to take (and a position which Leonard Woolf then took between 1923 – 1927). And despite Osbert thinking of ways for him to give up work at the bank Vivienne denounced his efforts, saying that he wanted to ensure that Eliot never escaped. And Vivienne dragged Eliot into her arguments with the Sitwells. Eventually she stayed in a nursing home to recover her nerves but when she returned home to a celebratory party she contradicted everything that Eliot said despite everything he stood by her.

However, these difficulties were not the cause of Eliot distancing himself from the Sitwells. He had already begun to do this for artistic reasons. He thought Edith was too much of an exhibitionist and considered Osbert's work to be in imitation of his own style. Osbert refuted any charge of plagiarism. But Eliot also thought Osbert was in the Georgian movement that was characterised by the "pleasantness" of the "insidiously didactic". And Eliot wrote in veiled criticism that; "The poets who consider themselves most opposed to Georgianism, and who know a little French, are mostly such as could imagine the Last Judgment as a lavish display of Bengal lights, Roman candles, Catherine wheels and inflammable fire baloons, vous, hypocrite lecteur."

Eliot remained friends with the Woolfs and had a great opinion of Virginia as a critic, respecting her views. Leonard wrote that "She told Tom that he had got into the habit of ending lines with a present participle; he had done it with great effect at the beginning of *The Waste Land*, and he was doing it again in this poem *(Ash-Wednesday)*. She thought he should beware of it becoming a habit. Tom said that she was quite right and that what she said was very useful."

Eliot's magazine *Criterion* gave him freedom to publish work that he liked and he was opposed to the old-fashioned "suburban democracy" of the late nineteenth century. Eliot encouraged Lewis, who in 1922 was at the first reading of *The Waste Land*, to submit work. The work that Lewis wished to submit was called *The Apes of God* an attack on the literary world and the Sitwells in particular. In 1924 Eliot published the work and this reinforced his separation from the Sitwells. This was consolidated in May 1926, when Vivienne sent Osbert and Edith a cryptic message from Rome, saying that she needed advice about an unspecified scandal. They delayed in replying and Vivienne told Eliot that they had spurned her cries for help.

Eliot was no stranger to artistic temperaments and had supported his close friend Lewis, despite finding him "independent, outspoken and difficult." He could see that he was "a highly strung, nervous man, who was conscious of his own abilities, and sensitive to slight or neglect." Lewis saw himself as a true artist who led everyone else. But he was in relative poverty and obscurity. He had fallen out with friends, publishers and patrons. By contrast Eliot was well paid and well known for his work.

Then in 1925 Lewis sent part of *The Dithyrambic Spectator* for publication in the *Criterion*. Eliot said it was too long and that "I have felt for some time that it would be in your own interest to concentrate on one book at a time and not plan eight or ten at once."

Lewis replied "I am an artist … draughtsman, critic, politician, journalist, essayist, pamphleteer all rolled into one, like one of those portmanteau-men of the Italian Renaissance." Lewis then accused Eliot of plotting against him and they fell out.

When Lewis complained to Ezra Pound in 1925 about his perceived bad treatment, Pound assumed it was caused by the Sitwells but Lewis replied that, "with the constipated Shitwells I have had no economic contretemps."

In an attempt to help Pound tried to get Lewis' work into a magazine called *This Quarter*. Lewis then replied that Pound had "no mandate to interfere when you think fit, with or without my consent, in my career. If you launch at me and try and force on me a scheme which I regard as malapropos and which is liable to embarrass me, you will not find me so docile as Eliot."

At this point Lewis had become paranoic and began editing his own magazine called *The Enemy*. Here he ridiculed other writers, including Joyce, Eliot and Pound.

The relationship between Eliot and Pound also became problematic. Eliot acknowledged Pound as more responsible for the Twentieth Century revolution in poetry than any individual, however Pound saw his role as even greater and called it the "Pound Era".

POUND'S MAGAZINE

In 1926 Pound created a literary magazine to copy the success of his fellow modernists. He called it *The Exile* and announced that it would appear three times a year until he got "bored with producing it" and it would reflect his personal taste. In contrast the *Criterion* was a broader literary magazine that would print work that Eliot did not privately like or agree with, as long as it was worth disagreeing with them. He advised Pound that finding contributors of whom they could both approve would be as likely as seeing eye to eye with a cross-eyed man. In response Pound thought that most of the people Eliot published were not worth agreeing or disagreeing with. That Eliot's criticism was "apple sauce" and was a bookish writing about writing in order to cater to the "feeble and brittle mentalities" of the English and to be seen "as arbiter of British opinion." And if this criticism came from envy it was reinforced in 1927, when Eliot became an editor at Faber & Gwyer (which became Faber & Faber).

Eliot was diplomatic towards Pound in print, but public attack of Pound came in 1927 from Lewis, who published *Time and the Western Man*. Lewis said that Pound's "fire-eating propagandistic utterances were not accompanied by any very experimental efforts in his own medium. His poetry . . . was a series of pastiches of old French or old Italian poetry, and could lay no claim to participate in the burst of art in progress. Its novelty lay largely in the distance it went back, not forward; in archaism, not in new creation." He added that "some inhibition has prevented him from getting that genuine naif (which would have made him a poet) into his work. There, unfortunately, he always attitudinizes, frowns, struts, looks terribly knowing, 'breaks off,' shows off, puffs himself out, and so obscures the really simple, charming creature that he is."

Lewis called him a "revolutionary simpleton," who flings open all doors-"whether there is anything inside or not" - as a purely dramatic and childlike gesture. However, at this time Lewis was so extreme that not only did he denounce Pound, Joyce, Eliot and the Sitwells but also himself.

NEW CRITERION

And so Eliot became the leading poet of the modernist (though not at this point a best selling poet) and became less reliant upon other literary figures to further his career. Virginia was upset when Faber brought out a collection of Eliot's work and a reprint of *The Waste Land* which she had offered to reprint and he hadn't told her. She accused him of being shifty and his character was assessed unfavourably by others. So Eliot wrote to the fickle Lewis of the enmity some people felt towards him.

By 1927 Eliot sent Humbert Wolfe (a best-selling poet, reviewer and high ranking Whitehall civil servant) a score of books of verse to review for what was by then called *The New Criterion*, a literary quarterly. Eliot wanted him to write a dialogue on George Moore for the May issue and invited him to dine to discuss the future of the paper. Humbert said "It is being converted from a quarterly into a monthly, though I can't believe it will survive many months ... I can't understand how a body so thin and white goes on living. My word if he were your husband you'd have cause to worry. I look positively robust and coarse beside him. He's had pneumonia twice, and my belief is that he has consumption. However, he's very bright and cheerful about *The Monthly Criterion* as it is now to be called."

At this point in the 1920s Humbert and Eliot were good friends and Eliot would write poem letters inviting Humbert to lunch. When, in 1927, Eliot converted to Anglican Christianity, he would have found support from Humbert who had converted from Judaism and for whom Christianity was a favourite theme. Lewis derided Eliot's conversion and Pound wrote "In any case, let us lament the psychosis of all those who abandon the Muses for Moses."

Eliot's backer for *The New Criterion*, Lady Rothermere, withdrew her support at the end of the year. So Eliot enlisted Humbert's help to find alternative financial support and they visited Arnold Bennett, critic of *The Evening Standard*, to finance the magazine. Bennett was in the back drawing room of 75 Cadogan Square with beautifully bound manuscripts of his novels behind his head.

Humbert described the scene "Arnold with his dark tuft, rising like Shagpat's Identical, myself dark and conciliatory, and T. S. Eliot, pale, cold and speaking slowly with his soft persuasive voice like a white kid glove. And I dare say we did want money. Why not? as Arnold himself would have said ..."

Bennett was not impressed by Eliot's persistence or his journal and Bennett wrote in his diary for Friday, 13 January, 1928: "T.S. Eliot and Humbert Wolfe came for ... tea to discuss with me the future of *the New Criterion* magazine. Their real object was to find out whether I would find capital. I showed little interest. *The New Criterion* is a dull production and always will be."

The journal was eventually saved by a fund set up at the instigation of Frank Morley.

Around this time many of the literary and artistic leading lights were compiled into a collection of 17 Ariel poems published by Faber and Gwyer, including poems by Sassoon, Edith Sitwell, Humbert Wolfe and Eliot. All the poems were illustrated by recognised artists such as Eric Gill, Paul Nash, Albert Rutherston and Charles Ricketts. However, Humbert was to outlive his usefulness and was dropped by Eliot.

And by the late 1920s Eliot had become dominant and his main rival to literary greatness was the more lightweight but hugely popular playwright Noel Coward, of whom he wrote dismissively in 1929 in *Dialogue on Dramatic Poetry* "I doubt that Mr Coward has ever spent one hour in the study of ethics."

Ch 7 : *THE FAÇADE* (1923-1925)

The Sitwells were great talent spotters, whether literary, artistic or musical. And you were asked to the Sitwells' because they thought you had talent or for your entertainment value.

And one such talent was Noel Coward, young, tall, slim and good looking, with dark slicked back hair. He dressed smartly and it was hard to tell if he was confident or arrogant. But easy to tell that he was mischievous, like a satyr. He was Grammar School educated and had spent a short time in the army and described it as "one long exercise in futility" and now he was a budding playwright and actor.

Osbert Sitwell invited Coward to a recital of *Façade,* a collaboration between Edith Sitwell and the composer William Walton, on 12th June, 1923, that the Sitwells were to give in the hired Aeolian Hall on Bond Street and "from which," Osbert told Coward, "you might get a few ideas." This led to a key battle in the history of literature.

Edith recited her poetry set to Walton's accomplished atonal music, which included dance rhythms of polkas, waltzes and foxtrots. She was hidden behind a curtain painted with a huge black and white painted face by Frank Dobson (who was the sculptor working on Osbert's bust). Poking through the mouth of this was a huge megaphone, called a Sengerphone, through which she chanted, her poems. Edith's voice shrieked forth, to discordant tunes, verses that were strangely beautiful.

Edith said that she wrote the poems "at a time when a revivification of rhythmic patterns in English poetry had become necessary, owing to the verbal deadness then prevalent. The poems tell no story, convey no moral. Some have a violent exhilaration, great gaiety; others have sadness veiled by gaiety: many are exercises in transcendental technique ..."

However, mixing comic songs with serious works didn't give her work gravitas. Osbert also recited some of the poems. And their disembodied voices intoning nonsense verses in a Hall with bad acoustics was taken by critics as a leg-pull.

Nancy Cunard and Virginia attended. Virginia wrote in her diary "I judged yesterday in the Aeolian Hall, listening, in a dazed way, to Edith vociferating through the megaphone." "I should be describing Edith's poems, but I kept saying to myself "I don't really understand... I don't really admire." The only view, presentable view that I framed, was to the effect that she was monotonous. She has one tune only on her merry go round. And she makes her verse keep step accurately to the Hornpipe."

Nor did it appeal to other Bloomsburies, like, Harold Nicolson, who found it a dreary muddle and who wrote to his wife, Vita Sackville-West, "I am quite sure that in 50 years from now no one will ever have heard of those frauds the Sitwells, any more than they will of George Robey."

And even its composer, William Walton, saw *Façade* as under-rehearsed and called it "a shambles" "that's the simple truth of it."

Only Wyndham Lewis, who had also been present at a private performance in 1922 at Osbert's house at 2 Carlyle Square, was complimentary, and that was just to say that it was "an improvement on the first performance."

It had been a hot evening and a tired audience was neither enthusiastic nor especially hostile to the performance. Osbert actually exaggerated the first night into a dramatic fiasco in order to create publicity which played up to the image of the Sitwells being eccentric, daring trail-blazers in the arts. Osbert said that they "created a scandal and involved all connected with it in a shower of abuse and insult" that many of the spectators jeered all the way through.

However, the critics really thought it was just a joke in bad taste, designed to shock and without artistic merit. And Edith saw the critical reviews as "gross public insult" and called her mockers "philistines".

The fireman of the Hall even gave interviews to the press in which he said that though the Sitwells and Walton were "barmy - they can't help it". What really hit the mark for press and public was that in the middle of the performance Coward had risen, ostentatiously, and walked out of the performance. He then began a publicity campaign against them saying that "*Façade* is the work of 2 artists too long out in the midday sun."

And Coward saw mileage in the joke. In 1923 he contributed what he said was "my little burlesque on the Sitwells" called *The Swiss Family Whittlebot* to the revue *London Calling!* at the Duke of York's Theatre. His short sketch was a send-up of the Whittlebot family of poets – Hernia, Gob and Sago, and was a skilful parody of Edith's verse.

Miss Hernia Whittlebot was "charmingly dressed in undraped dyed sacking, a cross between blue and green, with a necklet of uncut amber beads in unconventional shapes. She must wear a gold band rather high up on her forehead from which hang a little clump of Bacchanalian fruit below each ear. Her face is white and weary, with a long chin and nose, and bags under her eyes."

Her prologue was; "To me life is essentially a curve, and Art an oblong within that curve...My brothers and I have been brought up on rhythm as other children are brought up on Glazo."

"Oxford and Cambridge count for naught
Life is ephemeral before the majesty
Of Local Apophlegmaticism
Melody semi-spheroidal
In all its innate rotundity
Rhubarb for purposes unknown..."

At the end of the sketch the stage manager despairs of making her hear that she must finish and signals to the Orchestra to begin the next number. At which she takes out a megaphone and the Whittlebot family are finally pushed off stage whilst still playing and reciting.

"Really not unfunny" was Walton's verdict and others said that it was "quite funny" or "quite unfunny". The Whittlebots became more famous than the Sitwells and brought welcome publicity for Noel and an angry letter from the Sitwells.

Coward said; "In the first 2 weeks of the run I received, to my intense surprise, a cross letter from Osbert Sitwell; in fact, so angry was it, that I first of all imagined it to be a joke. However, it was far from being a joke, and shortly afterwards another letter arrived, even crosser that the first. To this day I am puzzled as to why that light-hearted burlesque should have aroused him, his brother and his sister to such paroxysms of fury. But the fact remains that it did, and I believe still does."

Their bitter feud was picked up by newspaper journalists and one wrote; "I hear that Edith Sitwell was very annoyed at the Noel Coward burlesque of her and her brothers in *London Calling!* and wrote a letter of protest after reading the papers, winding up very cuttingly: "As I shall be out of town for the next few days, I fear I shall not have an opportunity of seeing the show." But Miss Sitwell's estimate of the length of run has been falsified, for *London Calling!* has already exceeded the few days she gave it, and looks like being one of the hits of the season."

Coward's riposte was that he would be delighted to put a stage box at the Sitwell's disposal for them and all their followers and admirers for any time they cared to come to see the revue.

By 1924 his sketch was so successful that he was invited to read poems by Miss Hernia Whittlebot over the brand new 2LO Wireless Station. His first ever broadcast was a fifteen-minute reading of Miss Whittlebot's poems and Miss Whittlebot regularly appeared in the gossip columns. Coward wrote "Hernia is busy preparing for publication her new books, Gildea Sluts and Garbage. She breakfasts on onions and Vichy water." Or "Hernia Whittlebot, whose poems I quoted a short time ago, has now turned her attention to Christmas card greetings. I went to see her at the Duke of York's Theatre yesterday, where Mr Noel Coward explained that the poetess was resting after a heavy lunch which she had taken in order to attune her mind to the correct spirit of Christmas. One little thing which she dashed off after two helpings of pudding is called *Christmas Cheer*. It runs:

Snow and Pudding,
Life and Death,
Nothing,
And yet Everything.
For shame, Good
King Wenceslas !"

Meanwhile Edith could not bear the public mockery and became ill. She retired to bed with an attack of jaundice. And put off a performance of *Façade* at Oxford because Osbert told her that "probably little Coward's supporters (being far in excess of intelligent people in number) would flock to the performance to insult me." And both brothers cut Coward from their circle of acquaintances.

Despite the bad publicity it helped bring Sassoon and Edith back together. When Coward's skits on Edith made her ill she turned to him for help. Sassoon found Coward annoyingly effusive and he willingly gave help. She described him as "fantastically loyal" *whilst his friendship lasted* and "the most generous minded man she knew." And he was "one of the very first poets," indeed "one of the very first people" to "uphold her."

Edith, who said that her favourite exercise was to sharpen her claws on the wooden heads of her opponents, also counter-attacked. Coward's name appeared in her newspaper articles "The fierce light that beats upon the throne is nothing to that which shows up Mr. Coward .... Whose elephantine wit lumbers and scampers breathlessly after an emotion as frail and destructive as a clothes moth."

However Edith's attacks couldn't hurt him. He had enough money and publicity from the show to give him the time to write, direct and star in his more serious 1924 play *The Vortex* about dis-functional upper class relationships and drug addiction. He was becoming famous as a wit and even his clipped way of speaking, "like typewriting" became adopted by the upper-classes. The only person who could hurt Coward in the period was himself. This he did when he allowed the press to photograph him sitting in bed in a silk dressing gown whilst on the telephone. They then used this photograph to label him a "dope addict" like the character he played in *The Vortex*.

Despite the new fame Coward hadn't given up on his previous successes. And in 1925 he published *Chelsea Buns* a slim volume of Hernia Whittlebot's poetry. One critic remarked that, "One almost feels sorry for Miss Sitwell, even though she has been, in the vernacular, "asking for it" for years."

In the preface Coward wrote "In France, Hernia Whittlebot has been hailed and extolled even more perhaps than in England. … members of the Whittlebot "cult" may be observed wandering like contented spirits temporarily released from their narrow confines of ungarlanded graves, and in their shining eyes the knowledge that at last they have found the source of life's inspiration."

"There can be no two opinions about Miss Whittlebot's work. She has Steadily climbed the precarious ladder of Poetic Conquest, and from the height of her unassailable pinnacle she now bestows upon an eagerly expectant public this new proof of her iridescent genius."

"She scatters the tepid tea-leaves of Victorian Aspiration and Georgian achievement with the incisive *mesquinerie* of a literary Bonaparte."

"Nothing is spared the flail of her titulative satire. The carcaphanous charm of Harlequin and Columbine evaporates like withered potpourri before the oncoming hurricane of her merciless pen."

In the collection her poems are deflated by ridiculous mundanity, e.g. MRS. GIBBON'S DECLINE AND FALL

> "Sibilant apples glistering now
> In your mauve hands,
> Like priests that hold a tortoise to their
> mouth,
> And Macabre days of tan and blue
> Go hopping one, two, three.

Good God, it's time for tea!"

In 1925 it seemed like there was no stopping the rise of Coward. However, by 1926, he was suffering exhaustion, after touring America. And whilst in New York he wrote to Osbert. And Osbert told Sacheverell. "The brute wrote me a letter of apology"

In order to make sure that the persecution of Edith was not renewed Osbert telephoned Coward to insist that he must also send an apology to Edith. "The point is that he's just intelligent enough to realise his floater."

However, Noel wrote that Osbert actually came to see him in person and proposed "quite pleasantly that I should apologise to Edith publicly in all the papers. I gave him an old-fashioned look and explained gently that he was very silly indeed which he seemed to understand perfectly and we parted very amicably. It really was becoming a bore because he wasn't' being asked anywhere, poor dear, owing to my popularity being the greater."

Coward wrote a private letter of apology to Edith and though relations reopened they were not "very amicable." In fact, the feud only ended five years later with a typewritten note from Edith to Noel reading "I accept your apology."

Despite this Edith continued to be unforgiving to Coward for many years before moving on. And in 1937 Lewis described himself as Miss Edith Sitwell's *favourite enemy* and how "Once I shared that distinction with Mr. Noel Coward, but Noel Coward has somehow dropped out. Why? Oh, I don't know - I suppose you can't go on getting excited about *Cavalcade* forever even if you are Miss Sitwell. Then Mr. Coward has recently become a member of the Athenaeum. It's time to drop an enemy when he does that. Noel Coward is not an enemy of mine, I should perhaps say. In that capacity he belongs to Miss Sitwell, and I am not butting in. I had to make it clear why I should be the favourite, and not him, that was all. All the same, I believe I shall always be the apple of her eye-now Noel's dropped out."

In 1926 there was to be a more professionally managed performance of *Façade* at Chelsea's Chenil Galleries in London.

One writer warmly received it and another said it was a considerable success but F.R. Leavis still described the Sitwells as belonging "to the history of publicity rather than of poetry." And by the 1930s Edith was to concentrate on prose and novel writing as poetry could not pay her bills.

Coward tried to make a comeback in 1927 with *Sirocco* but it was a failure and was hissed off-stage. He persevered and in 1928 *This Year of Grace* was a success and his popular career flourished though without the unanimous praise of his literary peers.

The poet, critic and civil servant Humbert Wolfe was critical of Coward's success as being low-brow and lightweight, "…And in the theatre, as we know, dirty linen is not merely washed, but riotously mangled, in public. No class of society, except perhaps the manufacturers of the ingredients of cocktails, will feel themselves in the debt of Mr. Noel Coward." And Humbert later, in 1932 lampooned Coward in *The ABC of Theatre;*

"N
Is for Noel. His genius is not
deep thinking, but thinking a little a lot."

Ch 8 : *THE APES OF GOD* (1923)

Edith, Osbert and Sacheverell Sitwell were attacked on another front. In 1922 T.S. Eliot had encouraged Wyndham Lewis to submit work to the *Criterion*. So in 1923 Lewis sent Eliot some sections of *The Apes of God* which satirized most of his literary friends, including the Sitwells and Bloomsbury Group. He submitted with a warning to Eliot that; "should any of these fragments find their way into other hands than yours before they appear in book-form I shall regard it as treachery."

The Apes of God was published in the *Criterion* in 1924 and the full attack appeared later in a 1930 publication.

Edith said how the "temporary parting of the ways in Osbert's house caused Mr. Lewis, after three years' brooding on the subject, to believe that Osbert, Sacheverell and I are evil symbols of the decay of civilization, and to denounce us in a book called *The Apes of God* – God being, in this case, Lewis, although the only resemblance between that gentleman and his creator lay in both having brooded over chaos."

For Lewis the lower orders of the art-world "Ape" or imitate the true, divine creative artists. He portrayed the Sitwells as the "Finnian Shaw" family with Edith as Lady Harriet Finnian Shaw, Sacheverell as Lord Phoebus and Osbert as Lord Osmund a big Ape who was able to make Apery without needing to be paid for it. They were "God's own Peterpaniest family" of middle-aged enfants terribles who were talentless, pompous and self-admiring poseurs who were without commitment to the true values of art.

Harriet was desperate for fame and her poetry was "All about arab rocking-horses of true Banbury Cross breed. Still making mudpies at forty". When a literary editor arrives, "she made no pretence that she could not have wrung his neck here and now for not putting *all* the poems of the Finnian Shaws that they had ever written into his beastly anthology."

Edith suggested that the attacks may also have been because Lewis became resentful after he lost his only (and dirty) collar at Renishaw and felt unable to come down to dinner. She wrote that he felt humiliated over this and saw the Sitwells as "evil symbols of the decay of civilisation."

But it was not just the Sitwells that were attacked. Sassoon was Siegfried Victor, whose poetry was unadventurous, nostalgic, and traditional. And who only got inspired by writing against the horrors of war; "a beautifyyly carved statue, a little over lifesize but of the finest finish" "compiling an anthology of verse for the Under-Thirties."

Within the cast of characters there were some that Lewis respected but Lewis showed that respect in his own way. Roy Campbell was called "Zulu Blades" – a person of very mixed race. "Blades was the 'black beast', an evil neighbour: what with his upstart disrespect as well for his metropolitan betters since he had brought the hearty habit of the African outstations into their midst, here. His skill with women was natural, it was true he raped them like steers, he must be working off ten years' solitary confinement in the Veldt." Around this time Campbell was friends with Lewis and Eliot and had been friends with the Sitwells until their quarrel with Lewis. He fell out with them after Osbert turned him away from one of their dinner parties for not wearing evening dress. He left in a rage and it was 10 years before they became friends again.

Lewis also attacked non-literary figures who had supported him. Lewis had quarrelled with Sydney Schiff, an American banker and a generous patron of Lewis's work and an artist. Lewis wanted more money from him and Eliot had to be called on to resolve the dispute. Schiff was gracious about his subsequent appearance in *The Apes of God*, saying that if the Apes are those who "practice a little art themselves but less than the "real thing" then my work has failed as far as you are concerned and I regret it. But our personal relations have not been based upon your approval of my work but on my admiration of yours."

Lewis was still resentful and made Schiff feel that he, Lewis, was the real victim of persecution. In 1931 Schiff was sad that they were no longer friends and sent Lewis £75 for medical expenses. At which Lewis finally conceded that Schiff had behaved handsomely.

Despite any damage Lewis may have made to the Sitwell's literary reputations the work was probably more damaging to his own and was in no way as popular or damaging as Noel Coward's attacks. However, its shadow fell over the Sitwells for a long time and was published in a full version in 1930, 6 years after the first publication in *The Criterion*. The saving grace for them was that it was not easy to read with its mechanical view of human behaviour and a rigid technique that never brought its targets to life.

EDITH'S NEW ARTISTS

Edith moved on from Lewis and encouraged other new talent. For instance, she promoted the photographer Cecil Beaton and his career prospered. Beaton took photographs of the unusual looks and striking glamour of the Sitwells. He said of Edith that he admired"her etiolated, Gothic bones, her hands of ivory, the pointed, delicate nose, the amused deep-set eyes, and sullen wisps of hair…"

And in 1927 Pavel Tchelitchew painted his first portrait of her. She preferred his work to Lewis's though she still hung Lewis's on her walls. She had a close loving relationship with him without sexual involvement, which was partly because of her virginal spiritual quality and mainly because Pavel was homosexual. They continued helping each other and she was his muse, whose money and status helped his career, though she felt jealous of his boy-friends.

When, in 1930, rumours reached Edith that she was in a chapter of *The Apes of God* named "Lord Osmond's Lenten Party". She initially refused to read the book then read it and wrote; "A writer and painter well-known in London (I had sat for him nearly every day for a year seven years ago), having tried to make a personal conquest of me in vain, has revenged himself on me and my family… naturally because I am a lady, I cannot say, except to intimate friends, the reason for this attack.

Unfortunately the author of *"The Apes of God"* is also a great writer."

Edith felt that it was caddish for a man to attack "a lady". So she launched a counter-attack, describing how "My two brothers were faithful friends to him, I was loyal to him in the teeth of a good deal of opposition. He repaid us and the others who had been inflexibly loyal to him in *"The Apes of God"*. In this, incidentally, he more than hinted that I am a woman of infamous moral character."

Edith attacked Lewis personally; "This is all I can say at the present moment about Mr. Lewis, but one day when he has long been dead (I mean, more dead than usual), and I have passed my prime, I shall write the story of his life for those who may still remember him. And in it I shall show how every little fault and every little mistake made by this fundamentally gently and affectionate character is the result of the fear that engrosses him, the fear that he is not loved, the crushing impression that those on whom he has set his affections do not return them ...."

And she attacked him professionally, saying that she felt Lewis had "definite intellect", but that he had never created "a really satisfactory picture or book". In contrast she was very loyalty to Pavlik praising his portraits of her. He painted another portrait of her in 1931 before going off to Somerset and even when, in 1933, Pavel Tchelitchew found a new patron, the American poet Charles Henri Ford, Edith was still loyal to him. Though he didn't return any affection.

REVIEWS

In 1930 Campbell was one of the few people to defend Lewis. When *The New Statesman* gave him *The Apes of God* to review. So supportive was he that the editor R. Ellis Roberts rejected the review, saying "I find you take a far more serious view of its merits than I can, & indeed take Mr. Lewis altogether more seriously than I think is justifiable." Campbell told the editor to go to hell, and said *""The Apes of God"* is not only a novel; it is, in spite of some lapses in proportion, a brilliant novel."

Lewis visited Campbell in his characteristic black cape and hat. Lewis was grateful to Campbell for his support and wrote; "At a point in my career when many people were combining to defeat me"…"you came forward and with the most disinterested nobleness placed yourself at my side, and defended my books in public in a manner that I believe no other work has ever been defended."

Lewis expressed his sense of being persecuted and reacted by publishing Campbell's review, a reviewer's preface, R. Ellis Roberts' letter and also Campbell's letter to Lewis. The suppression of the review and Lewis's lack of recognition were condemned. Then early in 1931 Lewis asked Campbell to write a monograph about him and in 1932 the publishers Chatto & Windus also commissioned Campbell to write a book on Lewis. The book was completed but was not published as Lewis fell out with the publishers.

Campbell also lost many friends by supporting Lewis. However Lewis also had a degree of respect from the next generation of poets, despite the fact that in *The Apes of God* also attacked younger poets like Stephen Spender who was called "Dan Boleyn" "A beautiful, effeminate, moronic nineteen-year-old would-be poet and potential "genius"." Whose "confused and frightened behaviour reveals his inability to understand what is happening to him." The character, like Spender, had frequent nose bleeds. Spender forgave Lewis. Eliot felt that Lewis was "breaking butterflies upon a wheel." That Lewis "often squanders his genius for invective upon objects which to every one but himself seem unworthy of his artillery, and arrays howitzers against card houses." However, many of the young poets appreciated Lewis's influence and in 1933 W.H. Auden grudgingly admired Lewis's provocations in *A Happy New Year*:

> "The Sitwells were giving a private dance
> But Wyndham Lewis disguised as the maid
> Was putting cascara in the still lemonade."

These negative effects of Lewis's attacks were still being felt by the Sitwells and they wanted good relations with other poets so in the 1930s they took out a Newspaper Notice to pacify the other poets, announcing that "Miss Edith Sitwell and Mr. Osbert Sitwell have pleasure in calling a General Amnesty – this does not apply to habitual offenders."

COUNTER-COUNTER-ATTACK

In 1934 Edith was still fighting back and wrote on Lewis in her *Aspects of Modern Poetry* that he; "according to himself, is not appreciated, though he even goes so far at to apologise for any little brusqueness that may have been noticed: "I'm sorry if I've been too brutal, girls." Now, Mr. Lewis, not another word. Please. I beg! You know you ought not to spoil them. And besides, the pretty dears like your Cave-man stuff. For it is not often that they meet a real He-man…"

Lewis retorted in *The New Statesman* December 1934; "Miss Sitwell has built such a really enormous glass-house for herself in *"Aspects of Modern Poetry"*." And in *"Time and Tide"* that "these incorrigibly "naughty," delicately shell-shocked, wistfully age-complexed, wartime Peter Pans – dragging out of their old kit-bags for the thousandth time their toy "great men"…; their Aunt Sallies; their aviary of love-birds, toucans and tomtits; their droned-out nursery melodies, accompanying the plunges of old rocking –horses. A bit sad, a thought dreary, like all circuses that have survived – dominated, this one, but the rusty shriek of the proprietress…"

1935 January Edith wrote to Christabel Aberconway that Lewis had "taken refuge with the old ladies of *"Time and Tide"*, and from the shelter of their skirts, and amidst the atmosphere of lavender and old lace, is yelling defiance at me. What has infuriated him especially is my reference to the fact that he was 'formed to be loved,' to his sentimentality, and to his age! (He is revoltingly sentimental. That is the trouble.)"

In the 1930s Osbert also helped in the counter-attack of Lewis by making postcards of Lewis and placing them wherever he thought that Lewis might go, to play on his sense of paranoia.

Edith joined Osbert's fun and their practical jokes grew crueller. "When I feel cross, which is often, I tease WL. Osbert and I tease him without stopping...We also send him raving mad telegrams. I got one sent to him from Calais to his address in Percy Street, which ran thus:

"Percy Wyndham Lewis, 21 Percy Street etc. *Achtung, Nicht hinauslehnend.* Uniformed commissar man due. Stop. Better wireless help. Last night too late. Love. *Ein Freund.* Signed. Lewis Wyndham, 21 Percy Street."

And two days ago he got a telegram saying "*Achtung.Nicht hinauslehnen.* The Bear dances."

Both the Sitwells and Lewis were to become involved in Fascist politics, though Lewis was more extreme in his views and even wrote a book in praise of Hitler, so they knew that the joke would have particular impact on his senses of intrigue and suspicion.

But Lewis sought the last word and wrote in 1937:

"Osbert Sitwell I have always liked, rather in spite of myself- for those foxhunting men I can never really respect. ... But Osbert is a 'hearty' who has taken the wrong turning-he has looked at pictures, he has listened to music much too much-he has loved the Ballet not wisely but too well. I doubt if he could catch a fox to-day for all the equestrian aplomb of his patronymic.

Osbert was once a minor Maecenas. He has *le bel air* ... A Hanoverian hauteur and a beautiful lisp – which helped him out as a *raconteur*, and he was one of Chelsea's best. He threw quite a good dinner party in his salad days, and he was about the last person in London to mix 'mind' with his Mayfair."

"But Edith Sitwell is another matter. Edith-she is a poetess by the way-is a bad loser. When worsted in argument, she throws Queensberry Rules to the winds. She once called me Percy.

Although I don't like Edith quite so much as I like Osbert (she said I 'wanted to be loved' on one occasion, so I need make no bones about saying that I do not love her) for all that Edith does liven up the English literary scene considerably....the Sitwell family. They are one of my comic turns. I assure you that if the above seems to you a bit rough in places, it is nothing to what Miss Edith puts in, once we get into a clinch in the newspapers. ... But I'd a damn sight rather have Edith than those cowards' who skulk beneath a *nom de plume*, and peashoot you from ambush.)"

He added that Edith "is one of my most hoary, tried, and reliable enemies. We are two good old enemies, Edith and I, *inseparables,* in fact. I do not think I should be exaggerating if I described myself as Miss Edith Sitwell's *favourite enemy*."

Ch 9 : "THE JAWBONE" (1924)

Wadham College was not considered one of the elite colleges at Oxford. Its undergraduates were mainly not from prestigious Public Schools. They were from Grammar Schools and included students from a range of Jewish and American middle class backgrounds. During the First World War Wadham had been a recuperation centre where officers tried to regain peace of mind before being tossed back to the Western Front. This history was deliberately forgotten in the post-war hedonism of Oxford. But by 1923 this hedonism was fading for the politically engaged undergraduates who began to arrive.

One of these was Cecil Day-Lewis who was tall and thin with penetrating blue eyes and thick fair hair. He had fresh-faced school-boy good looks, with a scar on his chin (from where a carbuncle had been removed). He was reserved and shy but, dressed in mixed tweeds or flannels and tank tops, he came across as haughty and aloof. And his bearing and the expression of his mouth were supercilious and seen as "stuck-up".

One of his role models was Robert Graves who was nine years older than Day-Lewis and lived on Boar's Hill, just south of Oxford. Day-Lewis said, "I remember meeting Graves at the bus stop and deciding instantly that this was what a poet should look like: blunt-featured, shock-headed, with a butcher-blue shirt, a knapsack and a manner withdrawn yet agreeably arrogant." He added how Robert Graves was "percipient or charitable enough to detect some promise in my terrible first book of poems."

In 1924, in his second year at Wadham, Day-Lewis set up, with Rex Warner, a literary society for students to recite their latest verse or read their academic papers and discuss the work of poets. They named the society "The Jawbone", in tribute to the jawbone of an ass which Sampson used to kill and drive back the Philistines. They took a trip to Selfridges in London and bought a piece of jawbone and this became a mascot which presided over their meetings.

Influential and established writers were invited to give talks and recitals. And although Day-Lewis was secretary and then president of the Jawbone he let others introduce the speakers. He did not see making connections as a means towards establishing himself in the literary world. He had "neither the wish nor the intellectual resource to exploit them," and said, "I looked upon writing as a vocation, not a career."

However, one speaker who impressed Day-Lewis was Humbert Wolfe, an old boy of Wadham, a senior civil servant and popular poet. Day-Lewis wrote that Humbert was "one of the wittiest men I have ever met, a figure of flamboyance and panache." Humbert was then working in the Ministry of Labour and his ability to charm the workers' deputations prevented some national strikes. Humbert became an influence on Day-Lewis, who was grateful for his help.

Humbert's style influenced Day-Lewis's *Naked Woman with Kotyle*, written about the dancing figures on a Greek vase. Day-Lewis began to recite this serious work at "The Jawbone" but when he announced the title one of the members, Tom Hopkinson, exclaimed "Lucky chap, old Kotyle" and the work was punctured. And whilst he began to recite…

"She moved to the slow
Dance of supplication
Her body's flow
Was a moon in motion ..."

…it was clear that the work was not taken seriously and this, perhaps, marked the beginning of the end of his relationship to the style of work of Humbert Wolfe.

FROM GASWORKS TO RECTORY

A year later another young poet arrived in Oxford. W.H. Auden, was tall and thin with pale skin and smartly cut blond-hair. His small fine nose, small yellowish eyes and prematurely wizened features were off-set with large ears. He knew how to dress and acted like a statesman. Even when relaxed and smoking his pipe his clothes were impeccable.

Auden dazzled Day-Lewis. They would go on walks and Auden would wear his father's doctor's white coat or "an extraordinary black lay-reader's type of frock coat which came halfway down to his knees and had been rescued by him from one of his mother's jumble sales". He would also variously wear a clergyman's panama hat, a green eye shade or a monocle and carry a cane or a starting-pistol. Auden would pronounce on an equal variety of topics, from cinema being doomed as an art form, to ballet being banned, to music-hall as the worthiest art form.

For Day-Lewis this was an eye-opening experience and part of his slow development into adulthood. Auden widened Day-Lewis's reading of the poetic tradition and with his tendency to scowl he also taught Day-Lewis which poets to dismiss. One of whom was the previously admired Humbert, whom Auden called "the typists' poet".

And over these discussions the distinctive approach of Auden, Day-Lewis and a new generation of politically engaged poets began to emerge. The two poets still had distinct voices and there was always a competitive edge between the two, as Auden acknowledged in the verse-letter, written with ink and nicotine stained stumpy fingers with their bitten nails.

One of Auden's key ideals was to make poetry an instrument for social change and to look outward and not inwards like the Georgian poets. Day-Lewis also said that "The Georgian poets, a sadly pedestrian rabble, flocked along the road their fathers had built, pointing out to each other the beauty spots and ostentatiously drinking small beer in a desperate effort to prove their virility. The winds blew, the floods came: for a moment a few of them showed on the crest of the seventh great wave, then they were rolled under."

Although Day-Lewis had two poems, *Sonnet* and *Autumn of the Mood*, included in *Oxford Poetry* 1925 it was around the charismatic Auden whom a group of poets began to gather. And Day-Lewis was partly excluded from this group as he was not homo-sexual. Christopher Isherwood, who was part of the group would theorize with Auden on the role that the illegality of same-sex relationships had in shaping personality and literary output.

"Without these prohibitive frontiers," Auden wrote in *For The Time Being*; "we should never know who we were or what we wanted."

Auden had a physical relationship with Isherwood who claimed "for years we fucked like rabbits every chance we got,".

Isherwood wrote of himself "He couldn't relax sexually, with a member of his own class or nation. He needed a working-class foreigner." And Auden and Isherwood had a taste for young, working class men, especially foreign ones. They believed that they were following political ideals by creating comradeship across class and race barriers, however, their predatory behaviour was exploitative.

Auden connected poetry to the political, economic and social situation of Britain and sided with the strikers in the General Strike of 1926. Day-Lewis and Auden worked during the strike for the TUC. And some of Auden's relatives disowned him for this. Day-Lewis and Auden were disappointed that the workers' resistance (to their employers and to the Conservative government) had collapsed. A collapse in part negotiated by Humbert Wolfe.

After the strike they felt that they couldn't return to the insular world of Oxford. However, in 1927 they did return to their double lives in Oxford and would go for walks to the Oxford gas works and municipal rubbish heap in their tennis whites. And then would return, coal dust blackened, to lobster suppers at the Rectory.

In the summer of 1927 he and Auden committed their theories to paper in Appletreewick. Both sought a new poetic form and rejected the Georgians and the Modernists as well. Poets like T.S. Eliot, who coldly observed the world in despair and was more concerned with experiments in form. However, Day-Lewis recognised Eliot's importance and said that "It was left to an American to pick up some of the fragments of civilisation, place them end to end, and on that crazy pavement walk precariously through the waste land."

Day-Lewis sought a synthesis between Georgian Pastoralism and new forms of the Modernists. Using verse forms and not free verse (like Eliot), he wanted poetry to have a social and political context, and the resulting style was to engage in the world's issues in a largely traditional form.

That summer Day-Lewis had graduated and was determined to be a poet, but co-editing *Oxford Poetry* didn't pay the bills. He needed an income as the £5 he raised by selling his university textbooks soon ran out. He had no idea how he might earn a living, except "that never should I sink so low as schoolmastering."

He spent a few weeks in London where he tried, but failed, to land a job as assistant literary editor at *The Spectator*. He got a commission to write a book review for the *Westminster Gazette* but found the task impossible.

And so his father arranged for him to work in miners' welfare where he could be on the front line of industrial relations. A perfect source of inspiration for political poetry. But he would have to return to live in Edwinstowe, to a home that felt like a prison. And Day-Lewis had great unease, on visits home to his father's vicarage, at the social damage that the new coal mining development was wreaking in his home town of Edwinstowe. So he went to the interview in a dark-blue sombrero and floppy orange bow tie. He struck a pose and acted like he believed a poet should. He was rejected from the position.

So teaching became the only option left. He thought about working in a school overseas, either in Turkey or Japan, but became a school-master at Summer Fields, a preparatory school in North Oxford. It was a nursery school for Eton and other leading public schools and prided itself on its academic success. But the family who ran the school was frugal, though lived well themselves, and the buildings were cold and run-down. Its advantage was that it was close to Auden, who was still at Oxford. So he took the job and wrote, "I took the post with the feelings of a spinster, no longer as young as she was, accepting an unattractive and socially inferior suitor to get away from home."

Meantime, in 1927, Auden submitted poems to Eliot. The reply was that the work was not quite right but that he would be interested to follow its progress. This left Auden un-phased, as did, his visit to Wyndham Lewis in 1928 where Lewis couldn't see the merit of Auden's work. Lewis "found him a rather "fey" oriental ambassador: very crafty and solemn. Like an emissary of some highly civilized, perhaps over-civilized, power who considered something needed to be done about him."

Ch10 : CUNARD FALL & BLOOMSBURY RISE

THE CUNARDS

Nancy Cunard, who had set up *Wheels* with Edith Sitwell, had a "look" that was more famous than her poetry. She wore leopard patterned clothes, cloche hats or turbans. And had darkly rimmed sapphire-blue eyes and "scimitars of gold hair" cut short, dyed and curved in strands over her cheekbones. She was often in magazines and was famously photographed by Cecil Beaton and Man Ray wearing African bracelets from wrist to shoulder. Reputedly she was the inspiration of "half the poets and novelists of the Twenties". She inhabited expensive hotels and was interested in whisky, opium, jazz music and inter-racial relationships.

Her mother, Lady Cunard was a rich American patron of the arts and lived at 4 Grosvenor Square, and also at Nevill Holt, a huge mansion in Leicestershire. Many young, successful writers received invitations to dinner, tea or cocktails and at the Cunards they might meet the best-selling novelist Michael Arlen who was introduced as, "the only Armenian who hasn't been massacred!" Arlen was in love with Nancy and based his character Iris Storm, the heroine of his *The Green Hat* on her.

But the main literary figure who frequented 4 Grosvenor Square was George Moore, who was in his seventies and loved Lady Cunard hopelessly. His most popular novel was *Esther Waters* 1894 and although he influenced James Joyce he was a traditional writer. He admired French literature and Impressionist painting and had been painted by Manet. He would clinch arguments by saying "But I have known Manet!"

Some of the happiest days of his life were spent at Nevill Holt and Sir Bache, Lady Cunard's husband, took to him because he had been brought up in the country and had worked in a racing stable. However, sometimes, Moore "would be bored or exasperated by the stupidity of the other guests and would shock everyone with flippant and irreverent talk and would outrage the host at the head of the table." For example, he was a

Protestant and would launch into an attack of Catholicism even if Catholics were present. "You can't change God into a *biscuit!*" in reference to the communion wafer. "And what are they going to do in America when they bring in prohibition? Will they use coloured mineral water for communion wine, as mummers do on the stage?" Then he would poke fun at "the obscene state of marriage" or tell an overly risque story.

This displeased the hostess and she would reprimand him afterwards and would be so angry with him "that she walked backwards and forwards like a wounded panther,".

He was also reprimand for being late to meals. And once, when guests had been invited over to meet him at luncheon, a series of messages were sent to him upstairs in the Knight's Room, his private writing-room, to remind him of the time. He still did not appear and the meal was started without him. One of the footmen was sent and bring him down at once. The footman quickly returned, explaining that he had not been able to deliver Her Ladyship's message as Mr Moore kept bombarding him with questions about the village cricket match that he was watching from his window.

Some of the guests tried to fight back with what they termed "Moore baiting", but he would turn the tables on them and it was said of his Irish ancestors, "Scratch a Moore and your own blood will flow."

He was happiest when he could write undisturbed, play croquet with Lady Cunard and have long, intimate talks in the evenings. He felt himself to be in paradise and that; "Few men have seen their ideal as close to them and as clearly as I have seen mine,". "Very few have possessed all they were capable of desiring of beauty and grace; I have possessed more, for the reality has exceeded the desire."

But that had been a long time ago and now, in 1922, he would walk with Nancy around Hyde Park and dine with her in the evening. She lived in Paris but visited London regularly, and stayed part of the time with her mother. Lady Cunard admired Nancy's poetry and Moore reviewed it with praise but said that it needed working on. Moore felt inspired by Nancy to write poems about her and would also ask Nancy some of his standard prurient questions about her life in Paris. "Tell me about your lovers, my dear," and pleaded, "I wish you would let me see you naked" - a plea which she eventually succumbed to.

Although the Cunards had many friends, like the Sitwells, the Bloomsbury group didn't get on with them. And whilst many people spoke of Lady Cunard's 'frail Dresden china' beauty, and 'bird-like charm', Virginia Woolf called her 'a ridiculous little parakeet-faced woman'.

EDITH SITWELL AND THE BLOOMSBURIES

Virginia and Leonard Woolf's Hogarth Press began when Leonard won a prize in the Calcutta Sweep-stake. With this they bought a printing press and printed stories by Virginia, Leonard, T. S. Eliot, Robert Graves and several others in their house at Richmond. They did this just to please themselves, and until Virginia's *Kew Gardens* was well reviewed in the *Times Literary Supplement*. She ran downstairs and saw the door-mat deep in letters ordering more copies. To meet demand they farmed out the printing of a second edition with a local printer: and hence they became The Hogarth Press, which whilst small still managed to produce a few best-sellers.

Another key figure in the Bloomsbury group was the wealthy, titled, Vita Sackville-West, who she befriended in 1924 and was to become Virginia's lover. She had a slightly masculine appearance. Under her wide rimmed black hat and dark bobbed hair she had large eyes and an aquiline nose. She wore ornately fabricked jacket coats with a white shirt and check skirts, the latest designs of the Bloomsbury coterie.

Sackville-West considered starting a rival periodical to Osbert's *Art and Letters*. "I do so want to do something to stem the tide of Osbert Sitwellism and all that slovenly, slipshod beastliness. I hate worms, and Pierrots, and peg-top trousers and all the rest of that paraphernalia."

Sackville-West was snooty but Harold Nicolson, her husband, was more straight-forward. Nicolson worked in the

Foreign Office and also knew the politician Oswald Mosley from being 18 at Sandhurst. And when Mosley crashed in the war and was invalided Nicolson found him work in the Foreign Office.

Virginia first met Sackville-West in December 1922, and got to know them well in 1924. Virginia and Leonard stayed with them at Long Barn, near Sevenoaks, "with its butler, silver, Persian rugs, Italian cabinets, and all other modern conveniences." It was not far from her ancestral home, Knole, with its 365 rooms.

Virginia began to see a great deal of Sackville-West. "She was very handsome, dashing, aristocratic, lordly, almost arrogant. In novels people often 'stride' in or out of rooms; until I saw Vita, I was inclined to think that they did this only in the unreal, romantic drawing-rooms of the novelist-but Vita really did stride or seem to stride."

Back in London they were driven by Sackville-West on a summer's afternoon through the traffic. She was a flamboyant driver who, when she "put an aggressive taxi driver in his place, even when she was in the wrong, made one recognize a note in her voice that Sackvilles and Buckhursts were using to serfs in Kent 600 years ago, or even in Normandy 300 years before that."

Sackville-West was only really comfortable in a castle, whereas that was almost the only place Leonard could not be comfortable and described the situation; "Virginia, on the whole, liked rather more than I did the conventional opulence of the life and habitations of the wealthy English upper classes. But returning from a week-end at Long Barn, after describing the "opulence", she added: "Yet I like this room better perhaps; more effort and life in it, to my mind, unless this is the prejudice one has naturally ill favour of the display of one's own character.""

The Woolfs were connected with many literary figures and Edith Sitwell was keen to befriend them. In 1925 a typical tea at Edith's Pembridge Mansions included amongst others, Virginia, Edmund Blunden, William Walton and others. Allanah Harper (a tall, fair friend of Edith) thought Edith and Virginia were like "two praying mantis putting out delicate antennae towards one another." The conversation turned to Sackville-West's long poem *The Land* that had won the Hawthornden Prize. "It's not poetry," said Edith. "It would be entirely suitable for the use of farmers to help them to count the ticks on their sheep." Virginia who loved Sackville-West asked, "Edith, must one always tell the truth?"

And in her diary of May/June 1925 Virginia wrote "Edith is an old maid. I had never conceived this. I thought she was severe, implacable & tremendous; rigid in her own conception. Not a bit of it. She is, I guess, a little fussy, very kind, beautifully mannered....She is elderly too, almost my age, & timid, & admiring & easy & poor, & I liked her more than admired or was frightened of her. Nevertheless, I do admire her work, & that's what I say of hardly anyone: she has an ear, & not a carpet broom; a satiric vein; & some beauty in her. How one exaggerates public figures! How one makes up a person immune from one's own pleasures & failings. But Edith is humble: has lived in a park alone till 27, & so described nothing but sights and sounds; then came to London, & is trying t get a little emotion into her poetry – all of which I suspected, & think promising. Then how eager she was to write for the (Hogarth) Press, which had always been her great ambition she said. Nothing could be more conciliatory & less of an eagle than she; odd looking too, with her humorous old maids smile, her half shut eyes, lank hair, her delicate hands, wearing a large ring, & fine feet, & her brocade dress, blue & silver."

Virginia also liked Edith's brothers and their "goodnatured generalities" of after-dinner talk. "But why are they thought daring and clever? Why are they the laughing stocks of the music halls & the penny a liners?"

Edith's 1925 Hogarth Essay *Poetry and Criticism* showed that she was a Modernist against the Georgians. Leaving behind the pastoral tradition that began with Wordsworth but rather than move completely forward she looked for a tradition even earlier than the Georgians. And found an elegant and romantic

Elizabethan style that evoked haunting memories of her childhood.

And Virginia was interested in the work and wrote, "Nothing of the protester or pamphleteer or pioneer seemed in her – rather the well born Victorian spinster. So I must read her afresh."

Edith got her ideas from many sources and her ideas of "texture" in verse came when she visited Graves in Oxford in 1925. He met her at the station and couldn't carry her luggage because he had hurt his arm playing rugby football. They struggled along together and Graves made the unsympathetic comment that, "It's nice to see a fine strapping woman who can carry her suitcases." Edith wasn't pleased as they contained books, manuscripts and an eighteenth century brocade cloak. He went ahead with a bicycle. However, they remained friends and Edith got on with his wife in particular. They invited her to stay on another occasion but Edith declined as their children were not well, and she had a horror of illness. This refusal was to come back and bite her when the Graves left for Cairo later that year without saying goodbye. And when Graves dismissed the Sitwells in print in 1929 in *Good-bye to All That*.

Virginia and Leonard were publishing Graves' poems and one afternoon in 1926 Roy Campbell walked into Leonard's room at the *Nation*. He was swathed in a melodramatic great black cloak and wore a large black sombrero. He sat down, scowled at Leonard, who knew him only slightly, and then said in the voice of a melodramatic villain, "I want to ask you whether you think I ought to challenge Robert Graves to a duel."

Leonard was astonished and could only gasp, "But why?'

"Why?" said Campbell, "Why? Don't you remember the review he wrote of my book, the review you yourself published two weeks ago?"

Leonard had never thought there was anything in the review to "drive the most hypersensitive writer into lunacy." So for the next quarter of an hour he had to persuade Campbell that "the laws of honour and chivalry obtaining in Great James Street in 1926 did not require him to fight Robert Graves."

And in June 1925 Edith was at one of Virginia's parties and was asked to amuse her about Graves. Edith said that he was "like a high wind" which amused Virginia. Sackville-West was also present and Edith was embarrassed when Virginia asked her what she thought of the Rugby football school of poetry, that loosely included Sackville-West. Edith told Virginia that compared to herself they had led a sheltered life and could therefore hardly realise "how alarming it is to be pursued by flocks of enraged sheep ... trying to knock down and trample one underfoot, and to eat one's brains." Virginia noted that Edith "was like a Roman Empress, so definite clear cut, magisterial & yet with something of the humour of a fishwife – a little too commanding about her own poetry & ready to dictate."

Virginia saw Edith as "like a benevolent hawk, she pounces, she brings up the smallest treasure from the depth of one's mind and holds it til it glitters in the light." She saw Edith as having "a beautiful and delicate head, with large and delightful blue eyes, her birdlike delicacy of movement, her long and lovely hands add to the feeling of charm". And that "conversation with her reveals not only the beauties of her own mind but unexpected richness in our own."

Edith enjoyed receiving compliments whilst Sackville-West was not praised and "sat hurt, modest, silent, like a snubbed schoolboy."

And in return Edith was fascinated by Virginia's appearance and liked her but didn't like her work - though told her that she was one of the few living writers whose work meant anything to her.

However Edith was soon on the fringes, falling in and out of favour. In a letter to Sackville-West in 1926 Virginia wrote about Edith at a Bloomsbury party "sitting outside, with a glass between me and everybody, hearing them laugh: and seeing, as through a telescope (she looked so remote and washed up on a rock) poor Edith, in her brocade dress, sitting silent."

In this period Edith found a new supporter in the group, Rebecca West, who wrote that Edith "writes poetry as gay as a flower garden; its confused joyousness half heard through jazz music, as it is in the performance she and her brothers gave called *Façade*, is to me a great deal pleasanter than much of the confused passionateness one hears at the opera through the music of Wagner or Strauss, and surely just as legitimate."

When Edith sent Virginia a copy of her *Rustic Elegies* it interested Virginia so, in March 1927, she invited Edith to tea. Virginia saw her as "transparent like some white bone one picks up on a moor, with sea water stones on her long frail hands which slide into yours much narrower than one expects like a folded fan. She has pale gemlike eyes; & is dressed, on a windy March day, in three decker skirts of red and spotted cotton...All is very tapering & pointed, the nose running on like a mole. She said I was a great writer, which pleased me. So sensitive to everything in people & books she said. She got talking about her mother, blaspheming in the nursery, hysterical, terrible; setting Edith to kill bluebottles. "But nobody can take a liberty with her" said Edith, who prides herself on Angevin blood. She is a curious product, likable to me: sensitive, etiolated, affectionate, lonely, having to thread her way (there is something ghostlike & angular about her) home to Bayswater to help cook dinner."

And Virginia felt "Society here has become intolerable – save for ES (Edith) who was fascinating the other day – very beautiful – and full of astonishing stories about her mother's frauds: how she was made to catch bluebottles as a child and so on."

Virginia also used their friendship to make Sackville-West jealous (who was having affairs with many women including Roy Cambell's wife). Virginia wrote in letter of 23rd March to Sackville-West "I had a visit from ES whom I like. I like her appearance – in red cotton, many flounced, though it was blowing a gale. She has hands that shut up in one's own hands like fans – far more beautiful than mine. She is like a clean hare's bone that one finds on a moor with emeralds stuck about it. She is infinitely tapering, and distinguished and old maidish and hysterical and sensitive.... I like talking to her about her poetry – she flutters about like as sea bird, crying so dismally."

But the letter ends. "But honey can one make a new friend? Can one begin new intimate relations? Don't mistake me. No precipice in this case...."

Virginia's letter of 1927 July 24th to Sackville-West clearly shows an attempt to create jealousy. "I don't' think you probably realise, how hard it is for the natural innovator as [Edith] is, to be fair to the natural traditionalist as you are. Its [sic] much easier for you to see her good points than for her to see yours."

And in a letter of July 25th 1928 Virginia writes to Sackville-West "But ES is waving her hand – the loveliest in London – at me: she says I'm the only person she wants to know. Now how do you read 'know': it has 2 senses." The innuendo was clear but a complete distortion of Edith's friendship. Edith liked Virginia "You are one of the only people whom I *really* enjoy talking to." But did not sexually love her.

Eventually, by 22nd July1930, Virginia fell out with Edith when, shortly before leaving London for Renishaw, Edith gave a party at Pembridge Mansions. Virginia was amongst the guests and recorded in her diary. "ES has grown very fat, powders herself thickly, gilds her nails with silver paint, wears a turban and looks like an ivory elephant, like the Emperor Heliogabalus. I have never seen such a change. She is mature, majestical. She is monumental. Her fingers are crusted with white coral. She is altogether composed. A great many people were there – and she presided. But though thus composed, her eyes are sidelong and humorous. The old Empress remembers her Scallywag days. We all sat at her feet-cased in slender black slippers, the only remnants of her slipperiness and slenderness. Who was she like? Pope, in a nightcap? No; the imperial majesty must be included. We hardly talked together, and I felt myself gone there rather mistakenly, had she not asked me very affectionately if she might come and see me alone"

And however much the Sitwells may have wanted their family seat at Renishaw to become a place for writers to visit by 1930 this was not to be. And when in 1930 Osbert invited T.S. Eliot to Renishaw he declined, saying "It is indeed a long time since we have met, but I am not aware of that being due to any unwillingness on my part. On the contrary! I have thought of you often and wondered whether I should ever have a chance to see you again."

Meanwhile the Cunards continued to create their own literary empire with George Moore as part of the old guard. And on 5th December 1925 an unsigned review of Moore's book *Heloise and Abelard* appeared in the *Spectator*. It showered praise and insisted that Moore's work was superior to Thomas Hardy. Moore sent a copy to Lady Cunard, saying "Dearest Maud, I enclose an article from the *Spectator* which seems to prelude a new departure in my literary history."

This connection did little to further the Cunards' reputation. Moore was not liked by new writers like Edith though Virginia described him at a party on Tuesday, March 9th 1926 in a sympathetic manner; "He has a pink foolish face; blue eyes like hard marbles; a crest of snow-white hair; little un-muscular hands; sloping shoulders; a high stomach; neat, purplish well-brushed clothes; and perfect manners, as I consider them. That is to say he speaks without fear or dominance; accepting me on my merits; everyone on their merits. Still in spite of all uncowed, unbeaten, lively, shrewd."

Moore and Lady Cunard were linked to the Georgians and in 1928 Nancy, whose relations with her mother were very strained, left for France and set up the Hours Press at Chapelle-Reanville near Paris. Virginia advised her against setting up a printing press as "your hands will always be covered with printing ink." But she published work by Robert Graves, Ezra Pound and many others including Moore. And in 1930 she also published her own *Four Unposted Letters to Catherine* and *Twenty Poems Less* (1930).

Nancy remained a key literary figure and was painted by Wyndham Lewis in the 1930s. Her small press was one of many that were important to the modern movement as writers did not rely upon the public but rather were supported by patrons and a small elite readership.

Ch 11 : BEST-SELLING POET (1927)

Humbert Wolfe was debonnaire with the dark, handsome features of the Victorian Prime Minister Disraeli. His high pitched Oxford accent was as clipped and striking as his body language. Yet all this control and precision was crowned with thick, wild hair that was swept to the side in the manner of a Romantic Poet. In his strong, bony face, his brown eyes, surrounded with a ring of grey, had the look of a great comic performer yet they stared perceptively from behind his hawkish nose.

Humbert was a Principal Assistant-Secretary, the bright genius of the Ministry and British Representative at the International Labour Office of the League of Nations. He was well liked and known as The Chief. Amongst the old fashioned ministry men in their coats, winged collars and moustaches he was clean-shaven, wore an impeccable light suit, and an unmistakable bow-tie and carried a malacca cane. He scrutinized Ministers, Parliamentary Secretaries and Trade Union officials and deflated pompous fools with his deadly wit.

During the First World War Humbert had tried to enlist 4 times but was turned down on grounds of ill health. Instead he became the private secretary to Lloyd George at the Ministry of Munitions. And now he worked at The Ministry of Labour, Montague House, in Whitehall –opposite the Cenotaph and the entrance to Downing Street. The building was palatial and originally built for the Duke of Buccleuch. His armchair and double desk were huge, but dwarfed by the vast bay window and long curtains. His office was on the first floor, up the wide marble staircase and was formerly the library with huge bookshelves.

Humbert was uncommonly friendly with calculated impudence. Speech poured out of him as from a hydrant, while he sat back in his chair and stared out of the window. "People insist on telling me how to run the country, as though I were Prime Minister instead of a wretched anonymous Civil Servant slaving against his will!"

His popularity as a poet began with the publication of *London Sonnets* in 1920. Junior staff interested in literature would sit in an armchair beside his desk and discus the poetry of figures like Siegfried Sassoon, which Humbert declared was of prior importance to information that a civil servant was angrily waiting to take to a Minister, who needed it in order to answer a Question in the House.

Humbert seemed to be too clever by half, and was treated with suspicion by many high ranking colleagues in the Civil Service, including Harold Nicolson (Vita Sackville-West's husband) and whilst active in the world of letters, he would have nothing to do with Humbert 's books of verse.

As well as success in the Ministry Humbert gained increased literary success. In August 1922 he dined with Harold E. Monro, the publisher of the monthly periodical *The Chapbook*, associated with Georgian and Bloomsbury poetry. It ran from 1919-1925 and was produced from the Poetry Bookshop. *The Chapbook* contained a number of his poems in 1922 illustrated with a cover by Albert Rutherston (the younger brother of Sir William Rothenstein and a Bradford school-friend of Humbert).

Later that month Monro has asked him to dine on Sunday to meet a Director of Benn Bros, a new and rich firm of publishers, who made him an offer for his collection *Kensington Gardens*. The Director was probably Victor Gollancz - short, plump, middle-aged and balding. His cheerfulness framed with dark rimmed, round glasses and a well groomed moustache. He was well-dressed and with a restless, highly active mind.

He wanted to do them with special paper, and special printing and illustrated by Albert Rutherston. Royalties and possible sales were discussed, with the expectation of as many as 10,000 copies sold. Humbert held himself in, in case the deal collapsed, as so many other things had. And if *Kensington Gardens* was a success he planned to get the same people to publish his other things.

But Monro warned him against success. Humbert wrote how Monro "stood before the mirror in his little bedroom at the

Poetry Bookshop with his face of a mild, intelligent horse
looking at the reflection of another mild, intelligent horse. "You
don't run much risk of it," Monro mused, "to be fair to you. But
if you see it coming, hide. Think," he said, "of Arnold Bennett."

Humbert added, "Why when I showed him *Waste Land*
and asked him how he thought it compared with *Paradise Lost*
he said that he hadn't read *Paradise Lost*."

"It's all," said Monro, "the result of (his publications) *The
Old Wives' Tale* and *The Great Adventure*."

"His not having read *Paradise Lost*?" Humbert inquired.

"His not understanding Eliot," said Monro.

"Yes," said Humbert mournfully, "that is a high price to
pay for success."

"It is," said Monro "the highest."

Then, in September 1922, Humbert met Monro at the
Holborn Restaurant with Osbert and "Sacha". Humbert expected
to be in the *Spectator*, the *Sitwell Review* & the *Desk* poem. And
the following July (1923) Humbert dined with Osbert and
"Sacha" who were about to go abroad for six months. Osbert
gave him a copy of his latest book of verse and Humbert was to
edit together a collection of Sacha's verse.

And as Humbert became more popular and influential he
began to mix with Eliot and other literary figures, many of
whom he made light fun of. In 1925 he published *Lampoons* that
included the Bloomsburys.

Bloomsbury and Maynard Keynes:
"Confident that art and brains
end with them (and Maynard Keynes)
the school of Bloomsbury lies here
greeting the unseen with a sneer."

Meanwhile Humbert kept up his high profile job with The
Ministry of Labour. He got things done, hated bureaucracy and
promoted meritocracy including the equality between men and
women. He also humanized the pseudo-military treatment of the
hard at luck public at the Labour Exchanges. And helped keep

the nation sane during the General Strike of 1926. This was important work as by 1929 the Jobless total would rise to 1.5 million.

During this period Humbert was also a reviewer for the *Saturday Review* and also began reviewing for *The Observer* in 1926, when Viola Garvin became the Literary Editor. For his first review of a number of bad novels he "did an airy, wicked, naughty piece of writing which made us take him straight off fiction and reserve his charming mind and pen for books more in tune with them."

Garvin recalled the evenings of poetry in the Cafe Royal or in Soho when she and Humbert were joined by Harold Monro, reviewers, poets, publishers and their wives. "Then we used to adjourn to the flat, where Humbert lived at that time, in Mecklenburgh Square, where we argued and quoted nearly till dawn." This was a flat which he kept secret from his wife Jessie who he had sent to live in Italy with his daughter Ann. Jessie was a small attractive Scottish lady. She had a wavy bob, fine features under her cloche hat. She had a low waist dress with pleated skirt. She waited patiently for Humbert to join them in Italy as it was widely believed that he would be promoted in the International Labour Organisation in Geneva.

On 13 January 1927 he told Jessie that having agreed with Victor Gollancz on the edits to his book of poetry *Requiem*, it was now ready for publication. *Requiem*, was a eulogy to society's oppressed and the oppressors, the blessed and non-blessed. All of whom could be saved by Christ.

Humbert's reputation was growing, and on 16 January 1927 he went for tea at George Moore's house in Ebury Street. It filled with French pictures including portraits of himself by Manet. Humbert wrote to his wife of Moore:

"He is a very old man, though he has clearly never had a stroke. He has soft white hair, like fur, and the whole of his face is curiously on the slant to the left. He gives you the impression of having his head always cocked like a bird, though in fact he keeps it quite straight.

He speaks slowly with a soft Irish drag in his words, but his mind is as lively and as vigorous as ever. He spoke first of the very great pleasure a review I had done on him in "*The Observer*" some months ago had given him. "It wasn't", he said, "that it was pleasant to me, but it was written. I hardly ever come on writing nowadays."

"When he was showing me his pictures he showed me a little landscape of Mark Fisher. "Not a very good picture," he said, "but the man was born to paint you can see - as you were born to write." I was more pleased by that simple phrase than by all the other things that the critics have ever said of me .... "That's charming of you," I said, "but if it hadn't been for my wife, I'd not be writing now.""

THE BEST-SELLER

In May Viola Garvin reviewed his work for *The Observer*. He thought that it was the best he had ever had, & should start the book with a bounce. Sackville-West told him that *The New Statesman* was doing an early review but unfortunately Arnold Bennett was away, so his powerful assistance wasn't available.

Even Albert Rutherston's illustrious artist brother Sir William Rothenstein became enthusiastic about the reviews of Humbert's impending success. And in 1927 he wrote:

"My dear Humberto, I am told that the Bradford trade is not what it was. But I say that Bradford manufacturers are clearly at their highest. It is a particular pleasure to follow the steady crystallisation of your nebulae into a fixed star, the more so since for a time the world was grudging & ungenerous towards your gifts. But then I have always contended that we have to put gold under men's pillows in the night, while they sleep, lest we be arrested & cast into prison. Your new work, judging from the quotations in today's Observer, seems to me likely to move my bowels. I shall get it at once & be in your debt. Such debts, unlike others, are a lasting pleasure. Ever yours, Will Rothenstein."

Humbert was incredulous "Aren't they a marvellous family!" he wrote to his wife. "When you remember what he could have done for us! And then he speaks of the world being grudging and ungenerous. Well - can you beat it!'"

The publicity from the reviews was enough. Humbert 's *Requiem* appealed to Christians in a period when the fashionable elite had rejected faith in not only God but also in Man. It struck a chord in the period after the war. Other poets broke down tradition. But Humbert, the personification of tradition, became a celebrity. He was the decade's bestselling poet and the toast of the town.

He wrote how he spent "a melancholy lunch interval signing my name 275 times on the "de-luxe" *Requiem*." And in addition to the limited edition, they had sold a thousand of the ordinary in three days. Gollancz had been right to speak wildly of a best-seller its first week. And it then republished nine times due to high sales

No book of verse since John Masefield's *Everlasting Mercy* sold so well.

H.W.Garrod, former Professor of Poetry in the University of Oxford, called it "the most successful poem of recent years. For a vogue equal you will perhaps be driven back to that morning of February 1812 when Byron "awoke and found himself famous." And Humbert Wolfe enjoyed none of Byron's advantages of being a nobleman, wickedly romantic and widely travelled. He has had to contend not only with the temptations which his origins set him, but with the prejudices which they create. Recognition to Mr Wolfe came somewhat late; and I hope the more sweetly as from men who gave it grudgingly."

Garrod recognised Humbert as a singularly accomplished craftsman writing verse but also saw him as more concerned with sales than being as good a poet as he could be.

That Easter Sunday in 1927 Humbert had tea with George Moore to discuss the French translation of Moore's *The Brook Kerith* which Humbert said "is an amazing piece of work. I am reviewing it for next week's "*Observer*". G[eorge] M[oore] is trying to screw himself up to do a review of "*Requiem*". But I think that he'll fail at the post." And Humbert was correct as although Moore had liked *Requiem* he was going to try and get Sir Edmund Gosse to review it instead.

Despite the success Humbert had worries about his new publications as in 1927 Victor Gollancz "had quarrelled with Benn's and left them on May 1st. He had been in such a state that he has done nothing about the illustrations for Humbert's new book of poetry called *Cursory Rhymes* so Humbert was worried that it may be issued un-illustrated, however, Gollancz insisted on the author's integrity and allowed Humbert full control. Albert Rutherston's charming illustrations were included and *Cursory Rhymes* was a great success. And Humbert said "My dear Victor, no author has ever been luckier in his publishers, no man in a friend than I am in you."

However the work did not have a universal public appeal. One typist remarked as she saw him enter Montagu House in his Bohemian cloak and hat, that he was "a highbrow", whose poems exceeded her comprehension.

And Humbert's work was not liked by all critics. Robert Graves wrote in *A Survey of Modernist Poetry* 1927, with Laura Riding, that; "Never, indeed, has it been possible for a poet to remain unknown with so little discredit and dishonour as at the present time. The prima donna reputation acquired by Mr. Humbert Wolfe with work of the most crudely histrionic and imitative brilliance (his original comma-effects in *"Kensington Gardens"* began it) should not only comfort the obscure poet but drive him further into obscurity."

Graves' co-writer Laura Riding was a self-proclaimed prophet poetess from a New York Jewish family. She was pretty, with large dark eyes, a large nose, a strong jaw and a wide, flat smile. She had a pale complexion and held her head at a slight angle with medium length hair, too thick to be a bob. She wore fashionable, yet conservative, dresses with wide, frilly collars and matching scarfs. She had many emotional troubles and became increasingly unstable. And had had a breakdown whilst a student at Cornell University, when she was committed to a mental asylum for a while.

In 1928 Gollancz handled a solicitor's complaint from Graves and Riding to Humbert who had failed to name her as co-author when discussing a book they had written together. Gollancz wrote:

"Dear Mr Robert Graves,

(You probably do not remember it, but we met in the early days of the war in some little restaurant in Soho. It is clear from your letter that some condition of serious friction exists between you and Humbert Wolfe ... I give you my word of honour that I haven't the smallest doubt whatever that in the matter of the omission of Miss Riding's name he was innocent of any intention whatever to hurt. Miss Riding would, I am sure, be the first to admit that your own name is so much the more famous of the two that it is not unnatural, however regrettable the carelessness, to refer to the book under the name of the more famous collaborator..." ".... Forgive me for the length of this letter and for appearing priggishly in the very unusual role of peace-maker. But I know Wolfe well; and I felt I might presume on that meeting with a common friend years ago, to give you my very definite assurance that Wolfe, whatever his faults, is utterly incapable of consciously wounding anyone."

Riding replied with a lengthy letter of grievance against Humbert, complained that Victor had been rude not to write to her as well as to Graves and she said that his "wrongly inspired peace-making efforts" should be dropped.

In reply, Gollancz promised to drop the efforts but said that she hinted that he was an anti-feminist. "It may amuse you to know, therefore, that (a) the whole of my wife's family went to prison in 1913. (b) I, myself, had to keep in hiding at New College for three days because of a protest I made publicly on the river during Eights Week."

Despite such difficulties Humbert's literary reputation and circle of friends continued to grow. And in 1927 December 4th he attended a party thrown by the New York publisher George Doran in honour of Osbert Sitwell. Guests at the party included Noel Coward, Rebecca West, Ethel Mannin (a young writer and gossip columnist), and many others. They dined at the Pinafore

Room in the Savoy Hotel and for Humbert it was a meal of strange dishes washed down with a "wine that tasted like a Sitwell poem."

Mannin recorded how, after dinner, she went with Doran and Coward to Doran's sitting-room at the Savoy. Coward was in uncontrollable high spirits. He was gushing, calling everyone "darling," and saying "My deah!" and rhyming flagellation with adulation.

Doran warned them to be "ware of women with loose hips, because it generally went with loose lips." So Coward said "what "marvellous" words they would make for a fox-trot song or a revue number." He leapt up and danced around the room with coat-tails flying, chanting; "Loose about the hips, Loose about the lips."

Mannin also described Rebecca West as having flashing gipsy eyes and shining black hair. That she radiated light like a diamond, but not warmth. That she was "a brilliant mimic with mockery in her eyes and mouth, ready to speak about you as soon as you leave the room." Mannin wrote that West appeared to dislike more people than she liked and had "a mind like a sword-blade, and a tongue like a Whip."

Humbert became a close friend of T.S. Eliot and was a contributor to Eliot's *Criterion* magazine. Eliot would write poems inviting him to dinner. And Humbert became so confident in his success that he was able to give his honest assessment of his contemporary poets in *Notes on English Verse Satires* 1929 (published in Eliot's *New Criterion* and then by Leonard Woolf in the Hogarth Press).

He criticised the experiments in poetic form of Edith Sitwell and T. S. Eliot, writing that they "have not proved that the new form alone is appropriate to modern life, only that they have a slightly different way of achieving the old result, and in the oldest way of all- the imposition upon chaos of some wisp of order…"

And the war poets "…Siegfried Sassoon, Wilfrid Owen, Robert Graves and Osbert Sitwell began to present a picture of war which shocked all those who have never fought in it. But their work was, taken together, not so much true satire as invective and rebellion. They wished to expose the abominations of war, but they were too grimly in earnest to be able to use the weapon of ridicule.

Owen did not live to mature his vision. Robert Graves abandoned satire to devote himself to verse and to laying the foundations of a Critique of Pure Poetry, Siegfried Sassoon and Osbert Sitwell alone of that group' continued to develop the vein of satire. Neither has yet fully succeeded, though for different reasons. Sassoon's is too pensive and withdrawn a spirit for the service of this blunt drill-sergeant art. He will not rap out the words of command contumaciously enough, nor bully his thoughts into docility. Osbert Sitwell is far from suffering the same nostalgia that is forever drawing Sassoon back to poetry as he fringes the threshold of satire. It seems almost as though just before he drove the blade home he returned it to the scabbard, murmuring to himself "Are they, after all, worth it?" and perhaps even. "Is anything worth it?" It seems as though either he forgave his victims, or was disarmed by their ultimate defencelessness. But, satire does not permit its exponent to practice the virtues of a gentleman. It needs either a cad or a fanatic, and perhaps prefers a combination of the two…"

Wolfe then looks for the new champion of satire, leaving the reader to nominate him as the main candidate "…The best war-poets are either suggesting a retreat from spiritual agony into quiet, … or like Mr. T. S. Eliot …. commenting with despair but not with indignation on the atrocious muddle in which we are involved. Mr. Prufrock is not an invective but a lament. Edith and Sacheverell Sitwell draw further and further into a world accessible only to the light, and not to the darkness of anger. … let them pray heartily for a great satirist in verse in our time. For who (or what) else fights or can fight for us?"

Despite these criticisms of his contemporaries it would be a literary figure not on his radar, the writer and gossip columnist Ethel Mannin, who would create the difficulties between Humbert and the Sitwells that would lead to his downfall.

Ch 12 : HARDY'S FUNERAL (1928)

Humbert Wolfe first met Siegfried Sassoon on 25 September 1926 at the Holborn restaurant, when they dined with Monro. Humbert wrote; "He is quite the most beautiful Jew I ever saw. He is fair and tall, and very shy, and with only a tiny glimpse of the Jew in his queer otherworld face. He hardly talked at all, and he is plainly still deeply under the influence of shell-shock. O that devilish war!"

But as well as a fighting man Sassoon was a hunting man from a very privileged background and hunting created tension between the poets.

In 1926 Humbert wrote his poem *Sport at Minehead* for *The Saturday Review* about a horrible stag-hunting incident at Minehead. Humbert wrote that a "hind swam out a mile to sea, was pursued in motor-boats, & brought back by the hunt & given to the hounds to be killed! Isn't it unspeakably beastly! I don't know whether I can do the poem, but I'm going to have a damned good try this evening. I think it's the most revolting thing I've ever heard of in England - I mean so far as animals are concerned. When you think of the fat rich leisured people living round Minehead going out to indulge in an orgy of murder, it makes you despair of humankind."

> "The hunt is up at Porlock and the hounds are well away. (Satan, are you sleeping there below?) ... And the world is like a blessing, with the hunt at Minehead guessing it's a perfect day for slaughter, and by God! they ought to know."

But the chief source of difficulty between Sassoon and Humbert came out in their attitudes towards Thomas Hardy as Sassoon's dedication towards Hardy impacted on even his closest relationships. This was clear from his relationship with the Honourable Stephen Tennant whom he met in 1927 at one of Osbert Sitwell's dinner parties. Tennant was a friend of Nancy Cunard and both were decadent of society figures. He was a very thin, young artist with strong cheek bones and feminine features. He wore make-up and vests with flowers in open shirts and white slack trousers. Sassoon admired how he flaunted his homosexuality without worrying about how society reacted. And Sassoon pampered the spoilt, narcissistic and effete aristocrat. In his diaries Tennant wrote "You were beautiful this evening, Stephen, your hair and skin were lovely." And he was so out of touch that he posed for a photograph, at a time of increasing unemployment, in fancy dress with London workmen as a lark. Such antics caused resentment from the general public.

To celebrate their relationship Tennant commissioned Edith Sitwell's protégé, the society photographer Cecil Beaton, to photograph them. And they socialised within these artistic circles. However, when Tennant told Sassoon how much he had enjoyed meeting another of Edith's protégés, the painter Tchelitchew, in Paris. This made Sassoon jealous but did not go against any sacred idols.

Sassoon admired traditional art and poetry and wanted to share his artistic life with his lover Tennant and so, in 1927, took him to visit Hardy. Sassoon was deeply affected by what he called the "grim, wise fatalism" of Hardy's writing. "Since the war began I had taken to reading Hardy and he was now my main admiration among living writers." And this was Sassoon's last visit before Hardy's death.

Hardy was an important figure to many post war poets and writers. And T.E. Lawrence, an Oxford archaeologist and a war hero popularly known as "Lawrence of Arabia", also admired Hardy. So much so that even with a broken arm the reclusive Lawrence visited Hardy on a bicycle. And Hardy would play the composer Gustav Holst's *Planets* on Lawrence's gramophone when he visited him in camp on Egdon Heath in the Tank Corps.

Just as others admired Hardy, Hardy admired Holst, who was younger than him, but was still middle aged, wore spectacles and had short grey hair. He had the tired appearance of a bank clerk or bank manager, interrupted with joviality. On August 1927 Hardy took Holst for lunch and a motor trip, showing him Egdon Heath. Holst said that Hardy "was sorry I was seeing it in Summer weather and wanted me to come again in November." Holst then composed *Egdon Heath* as a homage to Hardy, saying, "Writing Egdon Heath gave me a new lease of life. As each fresh composition was written I felt I was beginning all over again. With a renewed strength and vigour."

Hardy looked forward to hearing the music but died in January 1928, 3 weeks before the first performance; in Paris, on a Sunday-afternoon. It was an excellent performance, but the audience hissed as soon as it was over. And the loudest of the hissing came from the people sitting immediately behind Holst. All his friends repeatedly assured him that in Paris it was a compliment to be hissed. Their consolation impressed him little and at the reception afterwards he drank three cocktails, one after the other. He hated cocktails, and this was the only time in his career that he chose to take this remedy.

After Hardy's death Humbert Wolfe published a poem in tribute of him which Sassoon described as a "trivial and pert little poem". It annoyed him, because he was the person who appreciated Hardy most yet his own tribute poems were rejected by *The Times* and *The New Statesman*. Sassoon thought that Humbert's popular verses were bad and infuriatingly mediocre and disliked how surprisingly easily Humbert got his work into print.

Hardy's ashes were to be buried in Westminster but his heart was buried in Stinsford Church, in the family churchyard, near their home in Dorset. Sassoon thought that Hardy should be buried in his entirety at Stinsford. And the whole affair drove him to distraction and made him hate the world.

And when Tennant, who had recently visited Hardy with Sassoon, didn't show any reaction to Hardy's death Sassoon became increasingly estranged from him and saw his shallowness.

On the 16th January 1928 Hardy's ashes were buried in Poet's Corner in Westminster Abbey. Sassoon arrived late at the Abbey and failed to reach his privileged seat. He watched the pall-bearers and the interment of the ashes from afar. And to add to his sense of injustice Humbert read one of his poems at the memorial service.

Members of the Bloomsbury group were also present and Virginia Woolf wrote in her diary on Tuesday, January 17th:

"Yesterday we went to Hardy's funeral. What did I think of? .... At intervals some emotion broke in. But I doubt the capacity of the human animal for being dignified in ceremony. One catches a bishop's frown and twitch; sees his polished shiny nose; suspects the rapt spectacled young priest, gazing at the cross he carries, of being a humbug; ... next here is the coffin, 'an overgrown one; like a stage coffin, covered with a white satin cloth; bearers elderly gentlemen rather red and stiff, holding to the corners; pigeons flying outside, insufficient artificial light; procession to poets corner; dramatic 'In sure and certain hope of immortality' perhaps melodramatic.... ... Over all this broods for me some uneasy sense of change and mortality and how partings are deaths; and then a sense of my own fame - why should this come over me? and then of its remoteness; and a sense of the futility of it all."

This sort of self-centred reaction led Sassoon to decry that the "Bloomsbury lack generosity." "I won't be "patronized and palavered over" by a group that thinks itself superior but lives in a tiny world. I sometimes think that they know next to nothing about life in spite of having read all the great authors."

And as Sassoon began to despise the literary world his book *The Heart's Journey* was published in 1928. Humbert was the first to review it and was, ironically, so lavish in his praise that, it boosted Sassoon's sales dramatically. Other enthusiastic critics followed. This indebtedness was greatly to Sassoon's embarrassment.

However, any warming towards Humbert chilled when, in *The Craft of Verse* 1928, Humbert provided a definition of poetry and considered that Hardy, who was judged to fail for want of music in his verse: "In a word, Hardy does everything except sing, and if that is true, he is everything but a poet."

Despite many admiring Hardy this wasn't universal and Rebecca West also felt Hardy was gloomy "One is apt to be discouraged by the frequency with which Mr Hardy has persuaded himself that a macabre subject is a poem in itself: that, if there be enough of death and the tomb in one's theme, it needs not translation into art... Really, the thing is prodigious. One of Mr Hardy's ancestors must have married a weeping willow."

However, Humbert was a repeat offender. Later, in April 1930, Humbert wrote an article about a new book on Hardy which he'd been sent. He thought that it was "utterly useless – silly little scraps from (Hardy's) diary, a pathetic record of the last years of his life." He foresaw a revaluation of Hardy. "I am surer every day that except for *The Dynasts* all his verse will disappear. His reputation will ultimately rest on *"Return of the Native"*, *"The Mayor of Casterbridge"* and *"Far from the Madding Crowd"*."

These supposed 'attacks' on Hardy, coupled with his sense of injustice over not being recognised as the champion of Hardy, would lead to Sassoon punishing Humbert.

Ch 13 : AUDEN & SPENDER'S PICNIC (1929)

In 1928 another poet entered the field. Stephen Spender, a young, handsome and agile undergraduate at Oxford. He wore tweed jackets and linen suits in a look of relaxed sophistication. And his ruffled hair combined with a quizzical expression was almost birdlike.

Spender had written an article in praise of Humbert Wolfe in November 1927 and readily admitted his own admiration as a schoolboy and an undergraduate was "fawning". He now wanted to develop his ideas about poetry.

He wanted to meet W.H. Auden, who was in his final year studying English, in Christ Church, a different college to himself. Auden could be seen around, sometimes carrying a cane and wearing a monocle. And they were introduced that summer at a lunch party given at New College by a mutual friend Archie Campbell. From this meeting Spender made an appointment to visit Auden, who saw Oxford University as a convenient hotel to stay, read books and entertain friends.

Spender arrived early and a "do not disturb" was on "the oak", the heavy door to Auden's room. He waited and finally entered to find the curtains drawn. Auden sat with a lamp on a table at his elbow shining at Spender. The light reflected back on Auden's pale face. His hair was almost albino and his light coloured eyes were set closely together as if he was squinting.

Spender wrote; "He jerked his head up and asked me to sit down. There followed a rather terse cross-examination in which he asked me questions about my life, my views on writing and so on. I tried to please, gave away too much, was not altogether sincere. "What poets do you like?" he asked again."

When Spender suggested Humbert Wolfe. Auden replied "if there's anyone who needs kicking in the pants, it's that little ass." Spender didn't defend Wolfe and also accepted Auden's view that "Siggy" Sassoon was "no good". And the dislike wasn't restricted to the less revolutionary poets, like Humbert and Sassoon. It included Wyndham Lewis and Roy Campbell because they were anti-gay. Auden then told Spender who was good. These included Wilfred Owen many others, and T. S. Eliot.

They drank coffee and during the meeting Spender became an uncritical admirer and a disciple. Then he was suddenly dismissed and told the interview was at an end. But their friendship was to develop. Spender was impressed by Auden's ability to recite poetry, saying; "He could recite poems with an intonation which made them seem obscure, and yet significant and memorable. He had the power to make everything sound Audenesque, so that if he said in his icy voice, separating each word from the next as though on pincers, lines of Shakespeare or of Housman, each sounded simply like Auden." And Spender said that Auden most loved poetry with this Audenesque "monosyllabic, clipped, clear-cut, icy quality."

Auden told him "that the subject of a poem was only the peg on which to hang the poetry. A poet was a kind of chemist who mixed his poems out of words, whilst remaining detached from his own feelings. Feelings and emotional experiences were only the occasion which precipitated into his mind the idea of a poem. When this had been suggested he arranged words into patterns with a mind whose aim was not to express a feeling, but to concentrate on the best arrangement that could be derived from the occasion."

Auden thought that the literary scene in general offered an empty stage. "Evidently they are waiting for Someone," anticipating that he would take the centre of it with his clinical approach to poetry with other writers around him. He was setting up a new group of British modernist writers. He was to be the leader of the "Gang", Cecil Day-Lewis was a fellow poet, Christopher Isherwood the novelist and, for a while, Spender the next poet/prophet.

Spender and Auden went for a picnic on a fine summer day. Spender described the outing; Auden "walked very fast on flat feet, with striding angular movements of his arms and legs and jerkings up of his head. Once he had been told by a doctor that he must walk as little as possible, so he immediately began going for thirty-mile walks. He had a theory that the body is controlled by the mind. He would explain a headache, a cold or sore throat in what are now called "psychosomatic" terms. We came to the open country, crossed fields and climbed a hill, where we opened our luncheon baskets and ate, lying on the grass."

Spender continued; "The landscape seemed polished by innumerable suns rising in the island sky, which seemed to have preserved intact through many centuries such a day as this, where two undergraduates lay in a high field, talking about poetry, as they might have done in Elizabethan times."

There Auden told him that Spender should not write poetry, but autobiographical prose narrative. And then began to describe his views on poetry; saying; "In a revolution, the poet lies on his belly on the top of a roof and shoots across the lines at his best friend who is on a roof-top of the other side . . . of course, at heart, the poet's sympathies are always with the enemy,".

He continued, "When he is in love the poet always hopes that his loved one will die. He thinks more of the poems which he will write than of the lover ... the tragic, at its greatest, is always funny." And one tragic-comic love interest that they were to share was for a fellow, undergraduate, Gabriel Carritt. Spender and Auden would write unrequited love poems about Carritt, who was heterosexual.

Auden also told Spender that he should drop the "Shelley stunt", adding that "The poet is far more like Mr. Everyman than like Kelley and Sheats. He cuts his hair short, wears spats, a bowler hat, and a pin-stripe city suit. He goes to the job in the bank by the suburban train." This suggested an influence of Modernism over that of Romanticism or Georgian poetry.

Spender also regarded Auden "as a kind of public entertainer. When he was amusing - as happened often - I laughed to the point of hysteria." "Generally he organized the people around him where he stayed to suit his whims, but he kept his hosts in a good humour. He was not witty. His humour was of a buffoonish kind and consisted partly of self-mockery. "I have a face of putty," he said, "I should have been a clown." Or, "I have a body designed for vice." He smoked, ate, and drank cups of tea all in great quantities." And "He was extremely particular about food, grumbled outrageously if everything was not arranged as he wished,".

In Spender's last years at Oxford he became Secretary of the University English Club, and organised the visits of distinguished writers who came to speak. And even though Spender's mind had been turned against Humbert Wolfe he was also invited. Spender wrote of his visit in 1929, describing how Humbert offered him some sympathetic advice;

"If you have a job in the Civil Service – which there is no reason you shouldn't have if you get a First like me – and if you are able to sell ten thousand copies, as I did of my last volume, you will be able to write poetry,". Spender said that Humbert "continued to talk of the books he had sold, in the transparent tones of one who buries his critics under his public." And Spender "began to realise now that the poet is, amongst other things, a man who has to have another job, tired, overburdened, who cannot live on his poetry and who is in danger of clinging to it out of self-esteem."

Wyndham Lewis was also invited to speak but he refused, however, he invited Spender to visit him in Ossington Street, which he did. And Lewis wrote "Spender, who is half a Schuster, and combines great practical ability with great liberal charm, showed me a lot of jolly poems, mostly about Auden – he said modestly, a much better poet than himself."

The two men did not get along, not least because of Spender's homosexuality. Spender later wrote defensively that; "Cambell, Wyndham Lewis and (now) Graves are carrying out a great campaign against homosexuals. They all attack them in writing and by wild and inaccurate gossiping. It seems that every modern writer who happens to be normally sexed, is so overjoyed to find himself normal in one rather unimportant respect, when he is wildly abnormal in all other ways (as are C,. W.L., and G.), that he must needs spend all his energy in attacking buggers."

When Auden graduated with a Third it was the least of his concerns. He needed to find employment and like Day-Lewis he worked as a teacher. His domestic comforts were "Spartan" and so, in early 1929, he left for Berlin whilst Spender was still at Oxford.

He soon returned from Berlin and stayed with Day-Lewis for a week-end of walking, music and eating. They considered the merits of contemporary poets. Owen and others were praised, Eliot was considered and Humbert Wolfe was criticised. And Auden "rapidly ate his way through our stock of provisions, his tremendous energy needing constant refuelling,".

Auden returned to Berlin and wrote an eighty-one line verse letter to Day-Lewis in March 1929 which included the lines;

> "While Wolfe, the typists' poet, made us sick
> Whose thoughts are dapper and whose lines are slick."

Later that year the new poets began to make some headway of their own. Cecil received a letter from Leonard Woolf accepting his first book *Transitional Poem* for autumn publication by the Hogarth Press. He at once despatched a card to Auden telling him the news:

> "Daffodils now, the pretty debutantes,
> Are curtsying at the first court of the year:
> Their schoolgirl smell unmans young lechers. You
> Preferred, I remember, the plump boy, the crocus.
> Enough of that. They only lie at your feet.
> But I, who saw the sapling, prophesied
> A growth superlative and branches writing
> On heaven a new signature."

Auden replied from Berlin "It is splendid news about the Hogarth Press. I liked the poem immensely and was duly flattered .... It's not the bad poets who are successful that one is jealous of, but the good ones like yourself whose medium happens to be a simpler one, because then one can't be superior about it. I am incredibly happy, spending my substance on strumpets and taking part in the white slave traffic."

Auden also had success with T.S. Eliot who published his *Paid On Both Sides* in the *Criterion* magazine. Eliot published it with reservations as he felt that Auden's mastery of technique was greater than his ethical or religious development but was the best poet he had found in several years.

Spender also made headway with Eliot. He wrote; "When I was twenty a friend had sent some of my poems to T. S. Eliot, and a few weeks later I met T.S.E. for the first time at one of those London clubs where I have met him so often since. His appearance was grave, slightly bowed, aquiline, ceremonious, and there was something withdrawn and yet benevolent about his glance. When Eliot orders a drink or inclines over the menu to consider a meal the affect is such as to produce a hush. It is a priestly act as he says in a grave voice: "Now will you have a turtle soup (I doubt whether it will be made from *real* turtle) or green pea soup?""

Spender disturbed him by announcing "I would like smoked eel."

Eliot replied "'I don't think I dare eat smoked eel," and Spender saw this as unconsciously paraphrasing Mr. Prufrock who in Eliot's famous poem asks: "Do I dare to eat a peach?"

Spender said "It is a fine day."

And Eliot replied gravely, "Yes, it is a fine day, but it was still finer yesterday," hinting in his voice that Spender was not choosing the word exactly. "If I remember, this time last year…" continued Eliot about the-weather and could not be easily interrupted. Spender later wrote, about the meeting, that "a few words of poetry would suddenly flash like a kingfisher's wing across the club room conversation."

Eliot asked Spender what he wanted to do. And Spender replied, "Be a poet."

"I can understand your wanting to write poems, but I don't quite know what you mean by "being a poet"," Eliot objected.

Spender said, "I don't only want to write poems, but also perhaps novels and short stories."

Eliot said, "poetry is a task which requires the fullest attention of a man during his whole lifetime."

To which Spender said, "I wish to be poet and novelist like, say, Thomas Hardy."

Eliot observed, "the poems of Hardy have always struck me as being those of a novelist."

This dismayed Spender and gave him a sudden insight that he could not devote himself entirely to poetry. He replied, "What I write are fragments of autobiography: sometimes they are poems, sometimes stories, and the longer passages may take the form of novels." And then asked, "What do you think is the future of Western civilization?"

Eliot replied, "politically there is no future "except" … "internecine conflict"."

"What exactly do you mean by this?" asked Spender.

Eliot replied, "People killing one another in the streets."

Spender could see the difference between their perspectives towards social and political action, and that Eliot looked from out of "a conviction of despair." Spender thought that Eliot's writing "confronted the breakdown of present values." That *The Waste Land* showed us the fragmentary nature of civilization, and that his later work *The Four Quartets* showed how our involvement in eternity frees us from the fragmentation.

In contrast Auden's poets had a different path to progress and peace. They were more conscious of a Marxist view of history, psychology and social class. They were Romantic but used common speech and praised science and technology. And Hardy was an influence for them. The Modernists like Eliot removed the personal from poetry. But Day-Lewis said "almost all of his [Hardy's] finest poems are nakedly personal". In particular Hardy's love poems written after the death of his wife Emma and his meditations on old age.

And it was this personal and political involvement that characterised the work of Auden, Day-Lewis and Spender but also brought them criticisms of being hypocrites.

Ch 14 : BLOOMSBURY TEA (1929-1931)

WOOLF AND WEST

In 1927 Virginia Woolf wrote *Orlando* a fictional biography of her lover Vita Sackville-West. Virginia wrote to Sackville-West "I dipped my pen in the ink, and wrote these words, as if automatically, on a clean sheet: *Orlando, A Biography*. No sooner had I done this than my body was filled with rapture and my brain with ideas. I wrote rapidly till 12."

It began in the sixteenth century England and travelled to the present day, with the heroine changing from one sex to another. In the novel there is an ominous, strangely prophetic account of a poet who came to stay with Orlando, accepting his/her hospitality and then writing a cruel satire on the visit.

When *Orlando* was published in 1928 Arnold Bennett attacked it in the *Evening Standard*. Virginia remembered this and her meeting with the critic Humbert Wolfe the next day at Eileen Powers.

They shared a packet of chocolate creams that an admirer had sent. And Humbert said "I am often asked if you are my wife. And I volunteer that I am happily married, though my wife lives in Geneva."

Virginia wondered why he protested and what was worrying him. But the meeting was brief and didn't produce a great review for her.

She wrote that he was "A theatrical looking glib man" with "a queer histrionic look in him, perhaps strain in him. Very self assured, outwardly. Inwardly lacerated by the taunt that he wrote too easily and deified satire." That he had blackberry eyes in a "sulphurous cavernous face".

It was Rebecca West who praised *Orlando* a few months later in the *New York Herald- Tribune* as "a poetic masterpiece of the first rank", and Virginia wrote her a grateful, happy letter, thanking her for a perceptive review of *Orlando*. West framed the letter.

Virginia met West over lunch in 1928 in Chelsea and described her as "most interesting, though as hard as nails, very distrustful and no beauty. She is a cross between a charwoman and a gipsy, but as tenacious as a terrier, with flashing eyes, very shabby, rather dirty nails, immense vitality; bad taste, suspicion of intellectuals, and great intelligence."

On their second meeting, Virginia thought that she looked as if she "has some bone she chews in secret, perhaps about having a child by Wells." H.G. Wells being the science fiction writer and social visionary with whom she had an affair and a son. She marvelled at Rebecca's animal energy and her fierce, outspoken talk: "R's great point is her tenacious and muscular mind, and all her difficulty comes from the weals and scars left by the hoofmarks of (H.G.) Wells."

And West, although untidy herself, was struck by Virginia's untidiness. She said "I always used to gain confidence from the sight of Virginia." Both looked overworked and rather ill and West though Virginia's face and body "could not have belonged to a person not of rare gifts."

Although the two writers got along, West found the whole Bloomsbury group "physically peculiar" and did not fit in, nor want to. She did not think that they liked her much either. Their style was too different. West liked demanding writers who were not afraid to commit themselves to "the large, simple, classic emotion."

Instead West preferred the Sitwells, who she saw as delightful and "among the few illuminants England possesses who are strong enough to light up post-war England"

BLOOMSBURY TEA

Orlando became a best-selling novel and marked a turning point in Virginia's career. She was the centre of the fashionable Bloomsbury group and Stephen Spender provoked intense envy and malice in fellow writers as he was welcomed to her meals with the group. He wrote:

"Sometimes I dined with Leonard and Virginia Woolf at their house in Tavistock Square. They lived in the upper half of this, the lower half being occupied by the offices of their publishing firm, the Hogarth Press. Their drawing-room was large, tall, pleasant, square-shaped, with rather large and simple furniture, giving, as I recollect it now, an impression of greys and greens." The panels were painted with images of mandolins, fruit and a view of the Mediterranean through an open window. There was a pleasant table of painted wood, the work of her sister, Vanessa Bell, who had also designed the dishes. West, incidentally, thought Bell's painted plates were "not good enough to feed a dog off."

"When her guests arrived, Virginia Woolf would be perhaps nervous, preoccupied with serving out the drink. Her handshake and her smile of welcome would be a little distraught. Now when I recall her face it seems to me that there was something about the tension of the muscles over the fine bones of the skin which was like an instrument tautly strung. The greyish eyes had a sometimes limpid, sometimes wandering, sometimes laughing, concentration or distractedness."

The dinner parties would go on until 2 a.m and she hated them to come to an end. She would be full of gaiety and tell slightly cruel stories about people that made her laugh until the tears ran down her cheeks. Then she would suddenly plunge into deep seriousness.

"Perhaps the name of a critic who ran a small literary magazine in which he had made a scurrilous attack on her would be mentioned, and she would say aciduously: "Why do you mention that name? Surely we have more interesting things to discuss." The uncomfortable moment passed and she answered, with a warmer interest, someone's question whether adverse criticism annoyed her: "Of course it annoys me for the moment. It is as though someone broke a china vase I was fond of. But I forget about it afterwards."

"She enquired of everyone endlessly about his or her life: of writers how and why they wrote, of a newly married young woman how it felt to be a bride, of a bus conductor where he lived and when he went home, of a charwoman how it felt to scrub floors. What bound people together escaped her. What separated them was an object of wonder, delight and despair....She seemed as detached from herself as from everyone else. Thus she would talk about herself with an objectivity which was unambiguous in her but which in others would have seemed uneasy."

Spender asked her how she wrote and she replied along the lines of; "I don't think there's any form in which the novel has to be written. My idea is to make use of every form and bring it within a unity which is that particular novel. There's no reason why a novel shouldn't be written partly in verse, partly in prose, and with scenes in it like those in a play. I would like to write a novel which is a fusion of poetry and dialogue as in a play. I would like to experiment with every form and bring it within the scope of the novel." Though she believed that prose was more difficult to write than poetry.

She demanded high standards of artistic integrity and Spender submitted a novel to The Hogarth Press which was rejected. She was interested in it and discussed it with him one afternoon, making several favourable comments. But when he asked how he could re-write it. "Scrap it!" she exclaimed. "Scrap it, and write something completely different." She continued, " No one should publish before he or she is thirty. Write till then, but scrap it or put it aside." Her method was to write reams of paper "just writing for the sake of writing," and then scrap it all.

Spender wrote that he also got to know T.S. Eliot who seemed "blinded to the existence of people outside himself", lacking connection or empathy. And who advised him that "I must always write exactly what I felt when I criticized his work and that our public relationship had no connection with our private one."

Spender described how, in 1927, Eliot told Virginia he would bring some "Jazz" records when he next visited her. And then, when he became a Christian with a profound sense of sin, he tried to show Virginia the significance of prayer. "To concentrate, to forget self, to attain union with God." To be absorbed in a peace and to heal the sense of shattering apart for one who has peered into "the abyss" of *The Waste Land*.

Spender's lack of belief in Original Sin divided him from Eliot, and his poetics divided him from Virginia Woolf, though they held similar political views; (hating Fascism and sympathizing with the Spanish Republicans). Virginia, however, objected to the way in which Spender, Auden and Day-Lewis put writing to the service of their views and were sold on account of their views more than the merit of their writing.

In the *Letter to a Young Poet* she criticized them for their impatience, their preoccupation with external social factors and their desire to set the world right. Feeling that they reacted to the problems of the world with their intellects and wills, before experiencing it fully through their sensibilities. "You have to be beaten and broken by things before you can write about them," she told Spender.

However, this kind of criticism couldn't hold the new generation of poets back. Spender considered that, like Eliot and Joyce, Virginia turned a hero into a passive spectator of a "civilization falling into ruins." He wrote that "critics like Virginia Woolf, who reproached our generation for writing too directly out of a sense of public duty, failed to see that public events had swamped our personal lives and usurped our personal experience."

Spender summarised their position. "The Georgian poets were a pre-1914 generation, the war of 1914-18 produced a generation of War Poets, many of whom were either killed by the war or unable to develop beyond it. The 1920's were a generation to themselves. We were the 1930's." And also "Rather apart from both the 1920's and 1930's, was the group of writers and artists labelled 'Bloomsbury'. Bloomsbury's has been derided by some people and has attracted the snobbish admiration of others: but I think it was the most constructive and creative influence of English taste between the two wars."

However, "Living in their small country houses, their London flats, full of taste, meeting at week-ends and at small parties, discussing history, painting, literature, gossiping greatly, and producing a few very good stories."

In contrast he saw "Our generation, unable to with-draw into exquisite tale-telling and beautiful scenery, terribly involved in events and oppressed by them, reacting to them at first enthusiastically and violently, later with difficulty and disgust."

And whilst Spender liked the "amusing conversation of Virginia Woolf," the "wryness of T.S. Eliot," and the "buffoonery of Auden," he wrote in more glowing terms about Edith Sitwell. That she: "had a power of invoking a massive and colourful historic past, whether of Egypt, Byzantium, early Christian mysticism, or the Elizabethans. Imagery of mature and golden ripeness derived from a profoundly personal existence.

She impressed all who met her by her presence, which was that of one of the survivors of a better and richer age....Her features seemed carved as though out of alabaster, in which were cut narrowly watchful eyes, amused, kind, cold, sad, or even at moments incisively shrewd. She wore magnificent dresses and large jewellery - an ivory cross, or jade pendant, or gold set with large and beautiful stones as in a bishop's mitre or cross. In her appearance, as in her poetry, she was triumphantly herself, yet endlessly reaching beyond herself into other people and   other   times.

We learned to appreciate the sensitive sympathy of Edith Sitwell. Her own well-being was bound up with that of her friends. After experiencing her generosity and sympathy, I was not surprised to learn that she had given up years of her life to nursing a sick friend. A more familiar aspect of Dr. Edith Sitwell was her humour, often revealed in repartee. One day, after a meeting of some gathering at which she had read her poems, a woman came up to her and said:

"Miss Sitwell, I just want to tell you that I quite enjoyed your last book of poems." Edith Sitwell looked at her remotely, and then, when she was about to go on, interrupted: "Now please don't say any more. You mustn't spoil me. It wouldn't be good for me to be spoiled.""

Ch 15 – PORTRAIT, HOLST & WOLFE (1927-1930)

Humbert Wolfe unlike some of the more progressive modern poets, didn't like Jazz, preferring ballet and classical music. And Gustav Holst, the composer of the *Planet Suite*, began reading Humbert's poetry in May 1927. *Requiem* moved him profoundly that a correspondence and a friendship soon followed.

Both took solitary walks around the parks of London at any hour (day or night). They found beauty in these spaces and in the lives of the city dwellers. And both hated anything slipshod, caring passionately for accuracy and detail.

Both had anglicised their names Holst had dropped von from it just like Wolfe had changed his name, from Umberto Wolff, to avoid being seen as German, the enemy.

And so, on Whitsunday 1928, when Holst read Humbert's poem *The Dream City* he felt as if it might have been written for him to set to music.

> ".. A silent square could but a lonely
> thrush on the lilacs bear to cease
> his song, and no sound else-save only
> the traffic of the heart at peace.
> And we will have a river painted
> with the dawn's wistful stratagems
> of dusted gold, and night acquainted
> with the long purples of the Thames.
> And we will have-oh yes! the gardens
> Kensington, Richmond Hill and Kew ..."

Holst enjoyed the deep and peaceful quietness of a London square, hidden from all the noise and confusion of the city. He had often looked down on 'the long purples of the Thames' from his window during the evenings. And he used to walk in Kensington Gardens in his college days, Richmond Hill had been an early mornings refuge for him when escaping the crying of his baby and he had always enjoyed Kew.

The Dream City became the first of the *Twelve Humbert Wolfe Songs* that Holst composed in 1929. And another of Humbert's poems that appealed to him most was *Betelgeuse*. This was about the brightest star in Orion of which Sir James Jeans had said: "If Betelgeuse were to replace our sun we should find ourselves inside it, its radius being greater than that of the earth's orbit." Holst had been reading about astronomy and would become so excited about the subject that his temperature would go up when he tried to understand too much at once, especially the ideas of the Space-Time continuum and distance in light-years. The effect in mathematics of the bracket on the minus sign was too much for him and he gave up algebra but continued his dreams of an expanding universe. And now, in these few lines of Humbert's, he found the insight he had been looking for in the books on modern science.

> "...On Betelgeuse
> the gold leaves hang in golden aisles
> for twice a hundred million miles,
> and twice a hundred million years
> they golden hang, and nothing stirs,
> on Betelgeuse.
> Space is a wind that does
> not blow on Betelgeuse,
> and time-oh time-is a bird,
> whose wings have never stirred
> the golden avenues
> of leaves on Betelgeuse."

The songs were first sung in Paris 1928 by Doroth Silk at a party given by Mrs. Louise Dyer, the founder of the Lyre-Bird Press, who had introduced *The Planet Suite* into Australia and had given a complete set of Holst's scores to the library at Melbourne. Holst was ill at ease in the midst of the distinguished gathering. But soon forgot his unsuccessful efforts to speak French as Dorothy Silk began singing the songs.

Three months later Humbert wrote to his wife Jessie from Geneva, asking if she was going to the first public performance at Wigmore Hall in London and "who the songstress was to be." Again it was Dorothy Silk. And *Betelgeuse* made the greatest impression as the audience held their breaths captured by the magic of those gold leaves that never stirred. But Holst had become so weary that he could barely listen. He felt numb as he had sunk into a cold, grey despair.

However, the works were complex and when Holst tried to published the songs they were initially refused by three publishers. Holst joked that it was like a renewal of youth to be having his manuscripts returned so frequently, and asked his daughter (Imogen Holst - also a composer) to put in a good word for him when she got the chance.

HOLST MEETS MOORE

Holst had been friends with Thomas Hardy and would become friends with George Moore, Humbert's friend, but Hardy's lifelong rival. When Hardy died Moore realised the triumph. He was well enough to sit up in bed and enjoy the perusal of the papers. He sat with straight white hair brushed across the skull and the plump pink cheeks, and the glacial blue of the eyes. For the moment he was the most venerable man of letters alive.

In the autumn of 1928 Victor Gollancz published Humbert's *Dialogues and Monologues*, a collection of seven essays, that included one on Moore which set out to correct the mistaken view that Moore was a half-serious and facile writer concerned only with style. Humbert was re-establishing Moore's reputation as against Hardy's. Moore's work had similarities to Humbert's as both were craftsmen whose apparently effortless word-control was actually the result of hard work. And Humbert became a close friend of Moore, and also a kind-of disciple.

Humbert idolised the elderly Irish poet and Moore's *Brook Kerith,* an imaginary tale of the days after Christ's supposed death, where Christ is not crucified but lives a full life, was the book that Humbert would choose to take on a Desert Island, if given the choice, but then would change his mind at the last moment in favour of taking the complete works of Shakespeare.

He admired this not least because Moore meticulously researched the work, including riding on a donkey from Nazareth to Jerusalem to get an understanding of the people and transport of the first century Middle East.

Humbert's devotion to Moore would lay him open to snipes of being a sycophant. In his critical study *George Moore,* published in 1931, Humbert gave admiringly, however, Moore took it as if entitled. And he also took Humbert's musical contacts. George Moore was to produce as a play of *The Brook Kerith* called *The Passing of the Essenes* and in 1930 wrote to Holst asking him to set a psalm to music: "I was so busy trying to get the things to fit together, to give everybody appropriate speeches, that I did not think of the music at all, saying to myself, "They'll hum a bit of plain chant as they cross the stage," and leaving it at that."

Holst agreed and was so scrupulous in his approach (even though he had only got to write one short chant) that he felt he ought to read the whole book before setting to work. So he bought *The Brook Kerith* from the nearest book shop and searched for a quiet place to read it. He finally chose Selfridge's roof garden and sat there for six hours.

They met many times and Moore talked of Ireland and painting among many other things. And when he gave Holst a copy of *Conversations in Ebury St.*, he wrote in it: "To Gustav Holst, with regret that this book does not contain a conversation with him - mayhap, who knows, another edition will."

But not everyone was as enamoured with Moore. Wyndham Lewis described Moore as an Irish literary clown. And Arnold Bennett told Virginia Woolf that whilst he had a profound admiration for Moore; he despised him for boasting of his sexual triumphs. "He told me that a young girl had come to see him. And he asked her, as she sat on the sofa, to undress. And said she took off all her clothes and let him look at her. Now that I don't believe ... But he is a prodigious writer - he lives for words. Now he's ill. Now he's an awful bore – he tells the same stories over and over. And soon people will say of me "He's dead." I rashly said: "of your books?" "No, of me." he replied, attaching, I suppose, a longer life than I do to books."

Moore died at 121 Ebury Street on 21st January 1933, aged 80. He left most of his items to Lady Cunard. On Moore's death Humbert's book was republished. The dust-jacket described Humbert himself as "a writer and poet of the first rank [who] deals with George Moore's works faithfully and in a spirit of sympathetic criticism."

Gustav Holst died the following year, on the 25th May 1934, of heart failure following an operation on an ulcer. He was aged 59.

POET LAUREATE

Despite any ambitions to the contrary Moore was not the pre-eminent Georgian writer of the 1930s. The new Poet Laureate was to have this title. In 1930 Robert Bridges had died and the Poet Laureateship was opened up. David Low's cartoon in the *Evening Standard* pictured all the possible laureates waiting to be interviewed by the Prime Minister. These included Rudyard Kipling, W.B. Yeats, Humbert Wolfe, Edith Sitwell, John Masefield, and Walter de la Mare.

The very elderly Kipling seemed the obvious choice, but was an impossible choice for the current Labour Government. Yeats was an Irish Free State Senator so couldn't be offered or accept the post as the King's poet. And Humbert discounted his own chance of being considered and consoled himself that "It wouldn't help me if I did get it. It would only mean deducting £100 from my Ministry of Labour income to take the place of the Laureate's £100 per annum."

There were protests that the Laureateship was an archaism which ought to be abolished. And *The New York Times* said: "The office itself has a beautiful absurdity ... But it is the peculiar wisdom of the English to value the absurd whenever it is also harmless." However, this didn't take into account that the

Laureate was not just expected to write verses for royal occasions. He had a real role in writing in a time of national problems and soaring unemployment. The Laureate also promoted the interests of English poetry and recognised poets as worthy of honour at a time when poets were being replaced by the stars of radio and Hollywood films.

Masefield was King George's favourite poet and was popular on both sides of the Atlantic. He had toiled in menial jobs in his youth and had never attended a university. And he was devoted to the cause of the common man, "the man with too weighty a burden, too weary a load". So England's first Labour Prime Minister, Ramsay MacDonald, wrote to Masefield, offering to submit his name to King George V as a successor to the recently deceased Poet Laureate.

Masefield, was 52, but looked older, with shoulders rounded as if he was bearing a weight of responsibility. He dressed smartly but modestly, like a doctor or shop keeper and had short hair and a moustache on small features. He wrote a letter in reply to the Prime Minister on 30 April 1930, and on 10 May 1930 the press swooped down to his house on Boars Hill, to the shy, simple, and gentle new Poet Laureate. Masefield posed for the photographers by a sundial and then in a field.

Masefield admitted that his appointment was the culminating point of his career. "While I am writing my poems I rejoice in the task. It is the work that is being done that appeals to me. But when it is finished I have no further interest in it. I never read it again, and the correction of proofs is a bore to me ... I take no pride in my work in the sense of keeping it in my mind and thinking about it. When it is done it is done."

These were the simple sentiments of a perfect Georgian poet returning to an ideal English simplicity.

Ch 16 : *THE GEORGIAD* (1931)

The anti-thesis of the Georgian sensibility was expressed by "the Zulu", Roy Campbell. He had a difficult time in the 1920s. In 1922 he had married Mary, a young, beautiful art student, without parental consent and his father cut him off. To continue living in London they had to pawn their wedding presents. And finally they had to leave and moved to Carnanonshire to find cheap accommodation where they could continue writing.

When Campbell's heroic long poem *The Flaming Terrapin* was published in 1924 it was seen as the antidote to the dry scepticism of T.S. Eliot and to the trivialities of the Georgians. He was seen as a full-blooded Romantic and the writer and war hero T.E. Lawrence said; "Get it – its great stuff."

In 1925 Campbell returned to his home country of South Africa and began lecturing on "Modern Poetry and Contemporary History". He became associated with the establishment of *Voorslag (Whiplash), a magazine of South African life and art* and wrote "Yet when we come to the end of the romantic period we come to the end of English literature. After the death of Byron we descend almost vertiginously through the later Wordsworth, Tennyson, Swinburne, Marris [sic] and Wilde till we land in the puddle of Georgian poetry."

England remained where literary reputations were made so he returned in 1927 even though they didn't have much money. Aware of his financial condition and talent the literary critic and Whitehall civil servant Sir Harold Nicolson and his wife, the writer Vita Sackville-West, invited them to stay at Long Barn, their bungalow in Kent.

Sackville-West was the daughter of Lord Sackville and her ancestral home, Knole, was a huge Elizabethan mansion, just 2 miles from Long Barn. Campbell accepted the invitation but felt that the Nicholsons' wealth and generosity, their silver, servants and spaniels were a reproach to his poverty. At their dinners he sat silent and downcast among their friends, whilst they talked about people he did not know and countries he had not visited.

Campbell disliked their academic discussions and prescriptions on love and felt that his own moral position was threatened by their coterie values. "I did not notice that he felt any resentment," wrote Harold Nicolson. "He just felt out of it."

When the Bloomsburies came to visit at Knole his wife Mary thought these were intellectual wolves in sheeps' clothing. "Virginia Woolf's hand felt like the claw of a hawk. She has black eyes, light hair and a very pale face. He (Leonard) is weary and slightly distinguished. They are not very human."

But one "fatal dinner", in the great hall at Knole, stuck in Campbell's memory and he put into his satire *The Georgiad*:

> "...I have sat like Job among the guests,
> Sandwiched between two bores, a hapless prey,
> Chained to my chair, and cannot get away,
> Longing, without the appetite to eat,
> To fill my ears, more than my mouth, with meat ...
> When I have watched each mouthful that they poke
> Between their jaws, and praying they might choke,
> Found the descending lump but cleared the way
> For further anecdotes and more to say." (CP,I,231)

His discomfort drove him to escape, without notice, to London to get drunk. Mary would return from the village shop to find their children alone in an empty house, doors and windows flung wide open. So she turned to a sympathetic Sackville-West for comfort. Sackville-West was only too willing to give this and soon Mary fell in love with her. They would meet in a lane near the cottage and began an affair together. Virginia knew of the affair and was intensely jealous, using her own relationship with Edith Sitwell to tease Sackville-West. However Sackville-West was not shaken. Her *British Georgics* was published in 1927 and it won the Hawthornden Prize.

When in 1928 Campbell discovered the affair. Campbell had had no scruples about his own love affairs but when his wife became involved in the sexual tastes of those at Long Barn and contemplated leaving him, he was deeply shocked and hurt. He ran away again, this time to go bull-fighting in Provence, France. Wyndham Lewis, a fellow pugnacious type, stayed with Campbell in Marsailles. And during a dull bull-fight Campbell jumped into the ring to take on the animal and was immediately knocked down. Lewis was inspired by Campbell and based barbaric contemporary characters on Campbell, who was pleased as it increased his fame.

Mary finally retuned to Campbell in 1929 and they both moved to France. There Nancy Cunard, who was not a friend of the Bloomsburys, published Campbell's *Poems* for her Hours Press in 1930 and it sold out.

Meanwhile, Sackville-West wrote less and less.

THE GEORGIAD

Campbell was also angry and sought vengeance on this affront to his manhood. So in 1929 he began an attack on the sexual immorality of the Bloomsbury Group in a long verse satire, *The Georgiad*, that took its form from Pope's parody T*he Dunciad* with its parallels to the savaging of the literary cliques of London. *The Georgiad* was directed at writers, reviewers and literary hostesses of the 'Bloomsberries' and especially Sackville West and her husband Harold Nicolson. They are grouped together as the Georgians' who have mutual admiration for one another's writing.

Campbell called Sackville West Georgiana and set the poem in their bungalow "Georgiana's Summer School of Love". An androgynous figure, Androgyno, enters the household but when Georgiana's husband Georgia is also attracted to Androgyno's amorous attentions she is horrified. The whole household sleeps with Androgyno and their activities include nude races across the garden.

Campbell laughs at these "young" poets, these Peter Pans who are "spry youths, some under ninety, I could swear, For two had teeth and one a tuft of hair."

Campbell saw *The Georgiad* as a kind of bull-fight and when visiting London he dressed in a toreador's hat and cloak. He saw bull-fighting as a noble sport of courage and virtues that was the opposite of a dull, pedestrian life. But he had no such respect for this literary adversary and called *The Georgiad* a 'Charlottade' after a mock fight in which Charlie Chaplin battles with a cow.

And whilst Robert Graves had also criticised the Georgians in his writings he was no ally of Campbell. Campbell attacked Graves for his dogmatic attempts to standardise and control literature intellectually. He felt that the upper-middle class academic poets like Graves were forcing their critical standards upon others; "…drilled, like Fascists, to enforce on all The standards of the middling and small …" (CP, I, 240)

Campbell also attacked Humbert Wolfe as representative of Georgian values. His roles as poet, reviewer and civil servant made him a perfect example of a writer tinged with middle-class amateurism. And Campbell disliked Humbert's popularity for writing the sort of poetry that he disapproved of. And whilst Humbert was not a Georgian, he was a reviewer, like Arnold Bennett and Harold Nicolson, who were Campbell's other main targets. Campbell, like Humbert, wrote for *The New Statesman* and the editor's decision not to print his review of Lewis' *Apes of God* in 1930 inflamed Campbell who linked Humbert to the values of the people who had rejected his review.

Humbert was described as: "More like a weeping willow than a man,! with trailing hair, as dreamy as a sheep,! and a great bow (to make the typists weep)."

And Androgyno, the hermaphroditic hero, would in Bloomsbury mode; "coo in satire gentle and polite! to fill the soul of Humbert with delight:" or growl and "startle Humbert from his dreamy stare! among the weeping willows of his hair,! whereon, I only wish it for the best,! he'd sometimes hang his harp up for a rest."

Humbert was accused of the Bloomsbury false humility: "until at last to Humbert's side I crawl/ and cower beside the humblest of them all," and of sycophancy: "And like poor

Humbert (whom I still pursue! in him addressing all your tribe and you) turn somersaults of such amazing daring! as dislocate both dignity and bearing."

It was widely known that Campbell was writing his satire so Humbert published a pre-emptive riposte called *The Ranciad* in *The New Statesman* in June 1931 before *The Georgiad* was published in October 1931.

Humbert did not identify Campbell by name, as he did not want to descend to personal abuse, but attacked Campbell's style and the satire consisted of a 78-line invocation to:

> "Divine Cacophone! ugliest of wenches
> at whose dread aspect all Parnassus blenches,
> .... Have I not also strayed
> by the Pierian spring, disgusting Maid,
> and spat into the waters, to ensure
> whatever else they are, they shan't be pure?
> Am I not willing with the rest to sneer
> at what in secret I respect and fear?"

> "Nor will I stop at that. My Muse shall curb
> the native insolence of noun and verb,
> seeking that happiest of all conditions
> when verse is one long string of prepositions ...

> ...particularly if it apes the stutter
> of a dead rat decaying in the gutter?"

THE GEORGIAD REVIEWED

Sackville West also made reply to Campbell's attack in an essay called *The Poet* in *Life and Letters*. In it the heroine meets a romantic and exotic young poet with wild eyes. The poet hypocritically claims that, "He never read poetry nowadays,... for fear of being influenced," "though, of course, he had read through the whole of English literature in his early youth". He dies of consumption, and, when she goes through his papers she finds that his poems are just copies and imitations of famous English poems.

Campbell's greatest ally was Wyndham Lewis who said that Campbell was a "pugnacious matador" and that *The Georgiad* was a "masterpiece of the satiric art, which may be placed beside the eighteenth century pieces without its suffering by that proximity." And whilst *The Georgiad* was less extreme than Lewis' *The Apes of God* both attacked "social" literary groups for their uniform mediocrity and artistic chit-chat.

But after writing *The Georgiad* the number of reviews of Campbell's work grew smaller. *The New Statesman*, which had published enthusiastic reviews of Campbell's *The Flaming Terrapin*, only briefly mentioned *The Georgiad* and then disparagingly; "The omelette of satire cannot be made without breaking eggs; but Mr. Campbell is mistaken in thinking that it is enough to throw rather ancient eggs at distant objects, and then tease them a little. The result is that dismal dish, cold scrambled eggs."

And the poem did nothing to help his literary social life. In 1931 Edith Sitwell described him as the "noisy frothing little Mr. Roy Campbell (that typhoon in a beer-bottle)". Virginia Woolf also criticised him in conversation to Stephen Spender. She told Spender that a poet had written a satire directed at Vita Sackville West and husband, whose crime was to have lent him for an indefinite period a small house in their garden where he might work. "What ungrateful people writers are!" she said. "They always bite the hand that feeds them."

But Spender gave *The Georgiad* good reviews as a masterpiece of satiric art. And whilst Spender rejected the Georgians he favoured a new style that was arising with the work of Auden's new group, whereas Campbell's disliked all "groups".

In 1932, one year after its publication the revenge that Campbell had sought in *The Georgiad* came back to haunt him. Mary took another female lover in their London home. And ironically only his fear of losing her finally drew her closer to him.

Ch 17 : *PINCHBECK LYRE* (1931)

In 1928 Siegfried Sassoon made his prose debut with the quintessentially English *Memoirs of a Fox-Hunting Man*. Edith Sitwell was disappointed that he had switched to prose and that he remained old fashioned.

In 1929 her long poem *Gold Coast Customs* developed her style and had an intense air of passionate horror and corruption. Yet, despite its success, she also switched to prose in an attempt to earn money. She was slaving over a biography of Pope when she had a quarrel with "the Aged old Earl" (her name for Sassoon) and felt that he deserved a good "ticking off".

She was hurt because he kept postponing an engagement to see her in Paris - with clearly fabricated excuses caused by his over-attentivenesss to his wealthy young artist friend, Stephen Tennant. But the tipping point came when a guest, who was an autograph collector had tea with Sassoon who showed the guest another writer's article about the Sitwells which described Edith as "Morbid, hysterical...out of touch with life...grotesque and nonsensical" and Osbert Sitwell was not even mentioned. On learning of this incident Edith wrote and gave the "Aged old Earl" "Blazes."

Edith was unable to forgive disloyal behaviour and said "I've asked him what the hell he means by being so disloyal as to disseminate abusive nonsense of that kind. I have told him Osbert, Sachie and I perfectly realise his attitude towards us, that we have understood it since last summer (the Siena Festival)." This referred to a row they had in Siena, Italy, at a Festival where *Façade* was presented.

Sassoon told Edith that he was determined not to quarrel with her and that he had only shown the autograph-collector the paper because it contained one of his poems.

And so he arrived for tea and gave her a peace offering; an expensive cigar box which he decorated with tinsel. Edith then accidentally caught herself in the lock, and thought that the box had trapped her fingers. This, combined with Sassoon's neglect of her and her jealousy of the relative success of Sassoon's relationship with his artist lover, Tennant, meant that any hope of reconciliation vanished.

Yet in 1931, when Edith ran out of money to pay her artist friend Pavel Tchelitchew, Sacheverell Sitwell was able to borrow £500 off Sassoon for her. After this she was warmer to Sassoon and wrote "His virtues are of an entirely opposite character to those of Mr. Lewis. He is home loving and extremely exact and tidy in his friendships (while they last – he is very changeable) are almost fanatically loyal. The bravery which made him so great a figure in the war is reflected in his appearance, and his is the most generous minded man I have ever known."

Edith and Sassoon disagreed on the merits of various poets. Sassoon thought that whilst the works of W.H. Auden, Stephen Spender, T.S. Eliot were "clever and adroit" they were deliberately difficult, obscure and allusive. However, they agreed that neither liked Humbert Wolfe, and had not liked him for some time.

Earlier, in 1927, at a party where Sassoon was present, Osbert had discussed the poetry of "Humbug" Wolfe which Osbert thought should be stopped. This was despite their work being so close that in 1927 the writer Somerset Maugham had thought that Osbert was just concerned with baroque architecture, Victorian bric-a-brac and the poetry of Humbert Wolfe.

And one of the games that the Sitwells played towards Humbert was recorded in 1930 when Ethel Mannin wrote in *Confessions and Impressions* said how Humbert once visited them in the 1920s at their mansion, Renishaw. When he arrived dinner was over and there was nothing to eat. To this "they said, "Oh, well, never mind," and showed him to his room and Edith came in and said should she read him one of her poems, and he said, "if you must," so she did."

Rebecca West wrote to advise Humbert to apologise to the Sitwells about having told people about the incident and to assure them that his spoken version would have been less condemning, however, this did not prevent the ferment that was brewing for an attack on Humbert for his attack. For Sassoon the tipping point had been when Humbert read one of his poems at the memorial service to Thomas Hardy and then went on to criticise Hardy's work. Humbert's good reviews of Sassoon's work did not counter the dislike. And in *Notes on English Verse Satires* Humbert had also said that Sassoon couldn't write satire as he lacked the lightness of touch. That he was too earnest. This proved to be fatal as Sassoon made a featherlike attack.

Sassoon supported Foxhunting, a sport Humbert hated - not least because he had once been caught up in a chase in his horse and carriage. Humbert quoted Oscar Wilde, that foxhunting was "the unspeakable in pursuit of the uneatable". And now Sassoon would be hounding him, egged on by Edith, not in a foxhunt but a Wolfe-hunt.

THE UNCELESTIAL CITY

So Sassoon returned to poetry one last time to attack Humbert 's latest poem *The Uncelestial City* published in 1930. The poem formed a journey of the soul that mixed Christian, pagan, and pantheist ideas, in a variety of lyrical, satirical and elegiac styles. It was original and was reprinted within the month - but the book was mauled by Arnold Bennett in *The Evening Standard* and by Harold Nicolson in *The Sunday Express*. Humbert was hurt and angered but felt no vindictiveness. He wrote;

"I wrote a longish book of verse called *"The Uncelestial City"*, of which Arnold (Bennett) did not approve. He was at that time king-making and unmaking in the Evening Standard. He signed the deed for my deposition from the thronelet I had briefly occupied in an obscure comer of Rabesqurat's kingdom. Proudly, I suppose, I had assumed my circlet of asses' ears and apes' heads, and not very much did I at the moment like the wrench when Arnold pulled it off. He wrote to me before the review appeared an affectionate letter saying that he felt it his duty to review the book, adding "Magnus amicus Humbert, major veritas." The review, following on a friendly little notice by Mr. Harold Nicholson beginning, "This silly little book", naturally damaged the book and hurt the author."

Humbert later reflected that; "There are writers who tell you that they do not read their reviews, there are others who prefer bad notices to good. Such men are either liars or more than mortal. In this matter at least I am neither one nor the other. I wrote to Arnold, approving his literary integrity but indicating only too plainly that I wished he hadn't used it at my expense. We exchanged several letters of increasing complexity and dignity. We did not meet for several months. He was busy and I was, I imagine, sulking. Then suddenly I heard of his illness. Like the rest of the world, I took it to be a bad attack of influenza, but I began to be worried at its prolongation. Finally I plucked up courage and went round to see him. When I went in the butler asked me if I would mind washing my hands in antiseptic. I felt suddenly cold. Antiseptic, what, why? At the very far end of an interminable passage I heard a door open, and I heard, faint, illegible and terribly changed, a voice that I had known whisper "Who is it?" "It's I, Arnold," I cried, but the door closed. It never opened again for me."

PINCHBECK LYRE

Sassoon, who disliked the Romantic motifs of love and death in Wolfe's work, saw his opportunity to finish the job that the critical attacks on Humbert had begun.

He wrote a collection of fourteen poems that parodied Humbert's work under the pseudonym of Pinchbeck Lyre. Pinchbeck was a cheap alloy that resembled gold and was used for Victorian broaches and the lyre was the musical instrument of poets in antiquity. And so the name suggested a fake poet.

Although he thought that it was funny Sassoon was initially reluctant to allow *Poems of Pinchbeck Lyre* to be published as he felt it was too easy a target. And its sub-title, *It is the season of larks*, showed it to be something of a public school-boy jape. However, 1,000 copies were published on 15 May 1931 by Edith's publisher Duckworth. 600 copies sold within the first 3 days and even though a second impression of 1,000 following almost immediately

In July 1931 Sassoon sent copies to his many literary friends, including T.E. Lawrence who requested extra copies. Sassoon wrote to his friends asking "Did you like "*Pinchebeck Lyre*? Unkind; but the result of much piffle-provocation."

Humbert was not prepared for Sassoon's attack and the effect on his sales was disastrous. He was stunned. But he forgave the attack. He wasn't angry or hurt, just sad that Sassoon, someone who he thought was a poet in sentiment and character, could be so full of hatred. And the book did little for Sassoon's reputation.

Sassoon was irritated by Humbert's sense of self-importance at the poet's power to immortalise his beloved, which usually started with Humbert's writing about himself. So Sassoon's *Conundrum* reads;

> "Which must be most immortal, which of us twain? –
> I, casting clustering assonances at you
> (And scribbling on my shirt-cuffs in the train),
> Or you, the ultimate indelible statue?"

And Sassoon's *Requiem* mocks the execution in *The Uncelestial City* with Humbert's often repeated "Swing dark, swing death!" replaced with Sassoon's "Swing tripe, swing tosh!" which was one of Edith's favourite opening lines from the collection.

Sassoon also criticised Humbert's interest in making money from poetry and said that Humbert's work would be forgotten.

Ironically Humbert's style was uncomfortably similar to Sassoon's own. His love of flowery adjectives meant that his over-written passages were similar to those he satirised. And Sassoon would lapse into the rhetorical devices that he ridiculed, such as making authorial asides, that interrupted the flow of the poem.

SEPULCHRAL EPIGRAM *(From the Greek)*

ONCE, stranger, on the windy
    Fleet Street plain
the brazen floral shindy
    I joined – for gain.
My harp's importunate prowess
    then could throb
where booming glory now is
    not mine to grab.
Too soon did poppied nightfall
    noose my ditties.
My fate was rather frightful.
    Nunc dimittis.

Meanwhile, Sassoon's and Humbert's real poetic enemies, the Modernists, were left un-assailed by the infighting.

Following Sassoon's success a 19 year old poet, John Gawsworth, attacked Humbert, again as Pinchbeck Lyre in *An Uncelestial Pity: Being a contribution towards a biography of the late Pinchbeck Lyre*. Gawsworth was a young man and a new breed of poet. And "John Gawsworth" was in fact a pseudonym for Terence Ian Fytton Armstrong. He had side parted, dark hair, a gaunt face, a long nose, thin lips and a tapering chin. He wore light suits and tight, slim ties.

His poem begins with "A grateful country raises a monument to him in St James's Park" and continues;

    ""Do not consider art or even immortality,
    Fame such as his outlasts all aeons of time.
    He is the poet consummate, don't you agree,
    Carven with loveliness, Byronic, sublime?""

But the tone changes;

    "And when with hushed Beauty the world is still
    And only the golden daffodil

Shakes ghostly petal at hyacinth.
Lyres profile glimmers from off its plinth –
Raucously Rima-d in the park –
(For the paint pot slinger a glorious mark)"

Undeterred by the attacks, Humbert published another volume of poetry in June 1931 called *Snow*. Again this was attacked by Gawsworth in a booklet of poetry called *Snowballs-Poems (Blue Moon Booklets No.9)*.

But Sassoon was not amused. He was outraged at the plagiarism of his pseudonym and said; "I only remember John Gawsworth as a schoolboy covered in pimples. And as a poet he is bogus. When I published *"The Poems of Pinchbeck Lyre"* he followed by producing two similar collections. This irritated me as it was plagiarism. But he says he never read the Pinchbeck Lyre book or even heard of it."

In 1932 compiled *Ten Contemporaries* bibliographies and essays on and by poets such as Edith Sitwell and he met Edith at an antivivisectionist meeting where some medical students started a fight and the two of them were shoved jointly out of the back door. She invited him for tea and for a time he became her "bun boy" at weekly gatherings, replacing Sassoon as her protégé.

Gawsworth deplored Auden's and Spender's work but also banished Georgian "moonshine" from his selections. Instead he created a movement of Edwardian poets (after King Edward VIII). The work was along the traditional lines of Tennyson and no modernist free verse was included. Unfortunately Edward VIII abdicated after wanting to marry the divorcee Mrs Simpson and so Gawsworth had to take the name of Neo-Georgians when George VI took to the throne.

THE REACTION

Humbert was still upset 6 years after the attacks and Edith wrote about when Humbert lectured with her at a Modern Poetry workshop in Cambridge in 1937, saying how "Umberto wouldn't speak to me because he thinks I've egged on Siegfried Sassoon."

One way that he tried to overcome his upset was to criticise modern poetry and position his work in the history of poetry.

In *Signpost to Poetry* 1931 he argued that "in contemporary poetry in the English tongue the fashion, if not the supremacy, is with such writers as the Imagist School,..., the Sitwell family, ... and Mr. Robert Graves among the British, and among the Trans-atlantic writers with Mr. Ezra Pound, Mr. Eliot, ... to mention some of the most distinguished or, as some allege, the most notorious....

...large sections of free verse are not poetry at all, and in consequence all those who have blindly followed his looseness without realizing remote harmonies are simply writing bad prose which cowardice in the critic and ignorance in the public permit to pose as poetry...."

"It is, of course, exceedingly easy to take cover behind these new forms and persuade the gullible or weak that rubbish of this kind is poetry:

But the fact that duffers use it to conceal their failure does not invalidate the community between these poets of purpose..."

"The truth is that T. S. Eliot is a dangerous guide. Though a thousand reasons of a psycho-analytic and quasi-metaphysical kind have been given why in *Waste Land* instead of a book he wrote a series of inspired chapter-headings, the fact is that he was too good a poet to write so on purpose. He did so because being T. S. Eliot he could none other, but it does not follow that other and younger writers, who do not happen to be Eliot, could and should do so...."

Then in 1933 he wrote in *Romantic and Unromantic Poetry* that;

"Nor can the three Sitwells be regarded as true revolutionaries ... All three of the Sitwells have, it is true, at times written technically free verse, but in essence it has always been tied to the strings of romance. Miss Sitwell, in particular, is almost savagely a traditionalist, except for her one whim, shared with her brothers, of expressing the objects of one sense in terms of another, a fantasy patented long ago by Rimbaud when he enunciated for all to know the colours of vowels."

After the attacks on him Humbert also sought a new creative direction, writing a play/ballet in three acts called *Reverie of A Policeman* which was published by Victor Gollancz in 1933. It was avant-garde and surreal and a departure from his traditional work. In it he considered his past and his future as a poet.

A policeman patrols the streets and sees through the walls into London houses where a Gentleman in Evening Dress and a Satiric Poet, both love a Ballet Dancer. The Gentleman destroys his love through jealousy and the Poet struggles against pessimism about love, poetry and the world.

Humbert is both the Poet and the Gentleman in a voyage of self-discovery of past errors. He learns to accept himself and find wholeness to allow for a new start. Which at the end of the play is for the Poet, to rip up all his work to date and to begin to write the play all over again.

As well as finding his literary direction Humbert was also swept into the urgency of his work. The jobless total in 1932 was 3.4 million. And to deal with the budget deficit Ramsay MacDonald's Labour Government was cutting unemployment benefits and betraying its working class voters. In this economic background Humbert became the head of the Employment and Training Department in 1933. He wanted to keep in touch with the general public and travelled the country to personally open the employment exchanges that he had set up and to visit the factories where jobs were being created or lost.

By 1933 Humbert started to write poetry again. And just as W.H. Auden and Cecil Day-Lewis wanted political poetry he sought the same and began writing satire against the rising Nazi menace. The hard economic and political realities had helped give him perspective. But his reputation as a poet of the past could not be shaken.

In 1933 Wyndham Lewis, who had become a Nazi sympathiser, published *One Way Song*. In this he praised his own power as superceding the like of Humbert, who is mentioned as one of the past establishment figures of poetry:

"Now come all ye who live in England's span
And tell me if I'm not a proper man.
A bollocky Bill, a mild-horned coptic ram.
And yet I'm all that is the sheer reverse
Of horsey He-man antics. Verse for verse
I can stand toe to toe with Chapman-or
With Humbert Wolfe or Kipling or Tagore!
I link my arm with the puff-armlets of Sweet Will,
I march in step with Pope, support Churchill.
The tudor song blossoms again when I speak.
With the cavaliers I visit, with Donne I am dark and meek.
With Cleveland I coin phrases-Inca buds
From a tree blasted. I am devout with Isaac Watts.
I am the genuine article, no doubt.
I drown my whispers in a libidinous shout.
I am hoarse with telling men to take more care.
P'raps that gives me my hoarse He-mannish air!"

Ch 18 : FASCIST OR COMMUNIST? (1932-1936)

The 1930's was a time of economic crisis, extremism in Germany and civil war in Spain. Communism and Fascism clashed and artists took sides.

In August 1931 the grounds of Renishaw, the Sitwells' family home, were opened for the launch of Sir Oswald Mosley's New Party. The Rally was attended by thousands. Mosley was a member of the British ruling class whose first marriage to the daughter of Lord Curzon was attended by King George V. Mosley had been wounded twice in the First World War and at twenty-three had become the youngest member of Parliament. In the 1920's Nancy Cunard was one of many society figures who stayed with the Mosleys. And at the start of the economic depression he had popularly called for nationalization of the banking system and government control of currency and credit. He was linked to fascism and these links grew to such an extent that Adolf Hitler attended his second wedding.

Mosley also had an affair with Osbert Sitwell's sister-in-law Georgia and Osbert joined Mosley's party. Osbert contributed to the party magazine, as did Vita Sackville-West, though his poems differed stylistically from the Bloomsburies and Virginia Woolf described Osbert's *Collected Satires and Poems* in 1931 as "all foliage and no filberts."

Wyndham Lewis also supported Moseley and did 2 drawings of him. Mosley said "Wyndham Lewis came to see me often in the thirties at my house." "He had the impression that association with me made him liable to assassination." However, Lewis was in favour of the individual and not Big Business and Big State and so was not in agreement with all that Mosley stood for. Still, Lewis shared a sympathy for fascism and made trips to Germany, even publishing a book praising Hitler in 1931. Lewis praised Hitler for wanting to end vice and homosexuality. And although Lewis had many Jewish friends, like Sir William Rothenstein, he was also ideologically anti-semitic, viewing the rich Jews as capitalist exploiters and the poor Jews as communist agitators.

Osbert also had Jewish friends but disliked Jewish people and Jewishness in general. He believed that the Jews had contributed to their own misfortune and he refused to accept the overwhelming evidence of Nazi atrocities against them, claiming that they had been scaled up by propagandists.

However, by far the biggest ideological supporter of the fascists was Ezra Pound. In 1931 Pound believed that poetry was connected to the ancient Greek Eleusinian mysteries that gave the male role model as either lover or warrior. As a young man in London and Paris he was the lover and now, in fascist Italy he took on the warrior role. Pound began dating his letters according to the fascist calendar, which began with the fascist march on Rome in 1922. He had contempt for the English except for Mosley's fascist movement.

In 1932 Mosley formed the British Union of Fascists and his followers, wearing black shirts, marched through London and attacked Jews, looting their stores and smashing windows in imitation of Hitler's terror tactics in Germany. Important supporters, like Lord Rothermere (whose wife had backed Eliot's *Criterion*) began to withdraw support. And it was also an extreme time in Mosley's personal life as in 1932 his wife drove to a casino, got drunk, danced to the shock of those present then smashed up her car whilst driving it home.

In 1934 T.S. Eliot openly caricatured Mosley's Blackshirts in his play *The Rock*. These new preachers of totalitarianism "firmly refuse/ To descend to palaver with anthropoid Jews". And they are presented as against the spirit of Christianity.

Eliot was Pound's publisher and that year Eliot warned Pound against Mosley. He also complained about the "obscurity" of Pound's "episstlary stile" and suggested his life's work *The Cantos* could be made more humanitarian. Pound wrote back to Eliot from Venice addressing him as the Right Reverend Possum Prodigious Wunkadorus Digwasher, urging the economics of social credit, and arguing that money should not be manipulated by financiers and bankers – which appealed to Eliot and despite political differences, their friendship continued

Eliot's friendship towards Osbert was more strained due to his opposition to Mosley. Their intellectual interests had also now diverged. When Eliot pressed Osbert for an article for *Criterion* he offered an essay on eighteenth century German architecture, on volcanic cities in Sicily or a story on murder or something to order. None of which were really suitable for *Criterion*. And although Osbert left the New Party in 1935 he still supported Moseley and the Sitwells had fallen from favour with Eliot.

When Edith Sitwell gave a cocktail party "une enorme reunion 'cocktail' at her club, *Sesame* in London, Eliot, wanted to see her before she went to America but he didn't like parties and wouldn't come. So, for her amusement, she kept sending him backdated messages about missed meetings, e.g. "My dearest Tom, what has happened? I stayed at home all afternoon waiting for you as was arranged. I hope that you are not ill?" the next day she would write him a letter dated last Saturday, saying; "My dear Tom, would you like to come and see me on Tuesday afternoon: unless you write to the contrary, I shall be waiting for you...""

In 1935 Osbert also showed support of Edith in the simmering family feud against Noel Coward by publishing *Penny Foolish*. Here he described Coward as a "competent but incomparably boring writer of musical comedies and revues" who "became a playwright, poet and musician." He had "less musical talent than Mr Adrian Ross, and less talent as a playwright than the late Henry Arthur Jones – both of whom were equally deservedly forgotten. We must not allow ourselves to be blinded by the fact that he does three things rather badly."

THIRTY PERSONALITIES EXHIBITION

Despite sharing fascist views the Sitwells remained enemies with Wyndham Lewis, whose views could be seen in *Paleface,* which was published in 1929, where he attacked writers whose work was "romantic", sentimental or passionate, believing that only reason, order or classical values could create great art or literature.

Rebecca West reviewed Lewis's *Paleface* in 1932 and said that he had a sparkling style and thrilling vision and that he detected trends of contemporary thought but was exaggerated and distorted. He appreciated the review and drew her portrait in 1932. In return, he admired her ability to withdraw herself from anything that repelled her and see it without passion.

He also drew portraits of Coward, who was a friend of West. And he said of Coward's sitting that "He came from Swiss Sports with a rush and a swing, of course, all suntan and Mayfair magic. The live-wire of the English Stage had a fine head. I have done Coward again quite lately but he then had become a Red Indian-still fine, but a bit Choctaw." He added that "I found that my women sitters were apt to dislike Coward. Of course he saw through them, and his actor's charm was too like their own. I believe in the end that Coward's career will rival, for sheer success, that of Sir James Barrie. He can no more help becoming a knight than I can help speaking Spanish when I want to speak German. He has not invented Peter Pan, that is true. But perhaps he has done better than that. He has *been* Peter Pan. That takes more doing."

The portraits, along with those of Eliot, Roy Campbell, Pound and Lewis were exhibited in his *Thirty Personalities* show in 1932 at Reid-Lefevre Galleries, in London. The private view was on Thursday 6th October. Lewis looked definitely odd as he wandered about in a hat, minus a front tooth. And after the general guests had left, he threw a cocktail party, for the "personalities" painted. One of these personalities was his constant supporter, Roy Campbell.

Lewis admired Campbell and tried to convert him to his own fascist views but concluded that Campbell "had no politics unless they are such as go with a great antipathy for the English "gentleman" in all his clubmanesque varieties; a great attachment to the back- Veldt of is native South Africa; and a constant desire to identify himself with the roughest and simplest of his fellow creatures in pub, farm, and bull-ring."

Lewis liked Campbell's stance against homosexuality and this fit with Hitler's promise to extinguish vice from Germany.

This was what had attracted W.H. Auden and Stephen Spender to Berlin, enjoying sexual licence. And Spender thought that because Germany had been defeated in 1918 the past customs had been removed so that youth could live again, without the inhibitions of Western Civilisation, and with a new hope and belief in humanity and brotherhood. In contrast Lewis praised Hitler's fascist structure for achieving reform without interference from the mob.

CAMPBELL IN SPAIN

Campbell believed in having a world of nobles and peasants and by 1933 he moved to a village in Spain. His poetry took on the themes of Mithraism, the religion of ancient Roman soldiers in which Mithras sacrifices a bull to bring the creation and salvation of the world. And writing on theses themes linked with Campbell's bullfighting.

Campbell drank a lot, ate and slept little. He had assumed that his income from poetry would be constant but it dwindled. And when the economic crash occurred and Britain abandoned the Gold Standard the value of his British money fell. And so his life in Spain, became like that of the threadbare peasants around them. And when his wife Mary converted to Catholicism he also converted. They worked hard and finally in 1934 Campbell could write to Lewis "I seem to have got into heaven – with no debts, nothing annoying or troublesome. But I had fierce time of it for some months..." He wrote that he was breeding "pigs and donkeys which I hope to sell to the British public as poets."

Both poets shared many interests and themes. Lewis worried about the blind progress of technology in *One Way Song* 1933 as did Campbell in *Junction of Rails* 1933-36. And Campbell saw it as "astounding how many ideas I have got the same as you" and Lewis called it an "amazing instance of Telepathy." But they differed in that Campbell wanted a return to the past and Lewis condemned returning to the past. Lewis saw himself as like a machine and told Campbell "My machinery still requires some adjustments – would that it derived not from protoplasm but some straightforward metal. But my health is pretty good." This described his illness in 1934-5 when he had surgery, to remove scar tissue from previous surgery, and had trouble with venereal disease from "juvenile inattentiveness to the dictates of sex hygiene come home to roost."

Lewis would end his letters with "Long live the New Spain!" And eventually, by 1936, Campbell followed Lewis and supported the Fascists in general because they thought that a bigger threat to Europe would come from the Communists.

For Campbell the Spanish Civil War was very real. In Toledo Campbell was caught between the warring factions as he did not want to be actively involved in the war. He was questioned by the chief of Police, part of General Franco's fascist government, and released as a foreigner but was told that, when the time came, he would be shot if he hadn't been shot already. The police then shot a gypsy who was Campbell's companion. And Campbell was put against a wall and hit with rifle butts so that his hands didn't work.

On the other side the Communist Popular Front had butchered and shot Priests and rich men. When the Fascist army began fighting the Communists near Alcazar, near Campbell's house. The richer men and the Fascist Toledo Garrison withdrew to Alcazar and the Carmelite monks called on Campbell to give refuge to their priceless archives. Campbell put the archives in a trunk for them. Later he found the monks, covered in tarpaulin, shot by the Communist militiamen. That same day the militiamen searched Campbell's house and leaned their guns against the trunk. Campbell had taken his religious items off the wall but had a copy of Dante's *Divine Comedy* on a shelf and was about to be shot for owning it when he showed some Russian novels to convince them he was not Catholic but was neutral.

Campbell believed that he and his family were miraculously spared. And as the towers at Alcazar burned that evening Campbell managed to escape with his family by bribing militiamen to let them ride in the back of a lorry carrying corpses. The lorry had a skull and crossbones on the side but as they crossed the Alcantara Bridge they were still put under fire by the garrison at Alcazar. Finally they arrived in a village, from where they caught a train to Madrid and then to Valencia.

APOLOGY TO GRAVES AND RIDING

The British Consul put Campbell on HMS Maine, a refugee ship bound for Marseilles. It was crowded with Britons fleeing Spain. Other passengers including Robert Graves and Laura Riding. Their meeting in this way smoothed over any resentment about the attacks that Campbell made on them in *The Georgiad* and an apology was accepted. Riding said to him; "Roy, you look starving. Would £500 be any good to you?" but his pride wouldn't let him accept it.

Campbell returned to England to headlines of "British Bullfighter Trapped by Rival Armies." And once again he had nowhere to live, but was lucky to be offered a temporary home at Marsh Farm, a house on a large estate in Binstead, Sussex. It was owned by the publisher Wishart, who had married Lorna, one of his Campbell's wife's sisters. The orchards were heavy with fruit. There was cream, butter, eggs and fresh vegetables. The linen sheets were clean. The baths were hot and the silver was polished. This all contrasted with the starvation in the Alcazar where the communists had sprayed petrol on the besieged building and tried to set it alight. Then they tunnelled under it and blew it up with charges.

Campbell disliked anyone who did not share his sympathy for the defenders and so his relations with Wishart deteriorated. Wishart supported the Left in Spain, and Campbell thought him perverse as he knew that people like Wishart were amongst the first to be shot in the Spanish Republic. Campbell wrote to Lewis "We are still in our 'Alcazar' in Bolshevik Binsted. I only wish you were here. Our hosts are trying to turf me out (my three brothers-in-law). I refuse to go – I am abolishing property and practically demonstrating their theories with uplifted fist – they send their ultimatums now by the chauffeur who laughs at them because they dare not come near here!"

English writers, he found, supported the Communists in Spain almost unanimously. Because he was convinced that a coming world war would be against Communism he thought that siding with the Spanish Republicans was siding with England's future enemies and that the Nazis were not the enemy to be feared.

Campbell wrote to Lewis; "I have seen enough of my old 'pals' to realise that they are a humiliated race and will coolie for anything that menaces them, instead of fighting it. All I like is those rattled old whores who are susceptible to Christianity. But I never had any sexual business with them. Only they used to give me food, and I would be a shit if I forgot them in their old age."

On trips to London he visited only low-life characters he'd known in his Oxford days, avoiding other artists. And so he felt more at ease with the poor and he felt ever more strongly that England was not his country.

That year, in 1936, Campbell brought out *Mithraic Emblems* his biggest volume of verse. It was ignored by all but the Catholic *Tablet*. And then he became a propagandist for the Catholic *Tablet* and turned a blind eye to Franco's brutality. This was followed in 1937 with his *Flowering Rifle* an epic poem that supported fighting in the Spanish Civil War and also praised Lewis.

NEW POETS

In contrast the Communist Left-wing supporters included Leonard Woolf. In 1932 his Hogarth Press had published *New Signatures: Poems by Several Hands* and Cecil Day-Lewis,

Auden and Stephen Spender were amongst the contributors. They used normal English Speech and imagery from contemporary life to associate with the working people, however, other poets in the anthology, like Julian Bell, who studied at Cambridge and not Oxford, said that Auden and Day-Lewis sounded like enthusiastic boy-scouts. And Graves also criticised Day-Lewis's political verse of the 1930s as having the sentiments of "a simple-minded Red" who had become too close to the "synthetic" Auden.

Spender was close to the Woolfs and would chat with Virginia in her drawing-room after dinner, whilst she smoked a cheroot. "There would be talk perhaps of politics, that is to say, of war. While Leonard was talking about war, labour, League of Nations, Virginia would fall silent. There was often after dinner this kind of political intermezzo. She had a little the air of letting the men talk: still more that of listening to Leonard."

And in 1934 Spender asked him; "Do you think there will be a war?"

He replied; "Yes, of course. Because when the nations enter into an armaments race, as they are doing at present, no other end is possible. The arms have to be used before they become completely out of date."

Spender described how; "Virginia had also a profound political insight, because the imaginative power which she shows in her novels, although it is concentrated often on small things - the light on the branches of the tree, a mark upon a whitewashed wall - nevertheless held at bay vast waters, madness, wars, destructive forces."

Spender said how the conversation passed from politics to gossip about personalities and that "Virginia had a passionate social curiosity, about the 'upper', the 'middle', and the 'lower' (I think these distinctions of class were sharply present in her mind). The Royal Family was a topic of intense interest to her. This preoccupation could be embarrassing - if one is embarrassed by snobbishness."

Lewis didn't like Virginia's self-absorbed position and on thursday, October 11th 1934 she wrote in her diary "A brief note.

In today's *Lit. Sup.*, they advertise *"Men Without Art"*, by Wyndham Lewis: . chapters on Eliot, Faulkner, Hemingway, Virginia Woolf ... Now I know by reason and instinct that this is an attack; that I am publicly demolished; nothing is left me in Oxford and Cambridge and places where the young read Wyndham Lewis. My instinct is not to read it. ...

Well: do I think I shall be among the English novelists after my death? I hardly ever think about it. Why t'shen do I shrink from reading W. L.? Why am I sensitive? I think vanity: I dislike the thought of being laughed at: of the glow of satisfaction that A., B. and C. will get from hearing V. W. demolished: also it will strengthen further attacks: perhaps I feel uncertain of my own gifts: but then, I know more about them than W. L. : and anyhow I intend to go on writing. What I shall do is craftily to gather the nature of the indictment from talk and reviews; and, in a year perhaps, when my book is out, I shall read it. Already I am feeling the calm that always comes to me with abuse: my back is against the wall: I am writing for the sake of writing, etc.; and then there is the queer disreputable pleasure in being abused - in being a figure, in being a martyr, and so on."

However, the criticism made an impact despite her attempts to ignore it and the following year, Saturday 16th March 1935, she wrote "... Bloomsbury is ridiculed; and I am dismissed with it. I didn't read W. L.: ... How resilient I am; and how fatalistic now; and how little I mind and how much; and how good my novel is; and how tired I am this morning; and how I like praise; and how full of ideas I am; and Tom (Eliot) and Stephen' (Spender) came to tea... My head is numb today and I - can scarcely read Osbert on Brighton, let alone Dante...

I'm thinking whether, if I write about Roger, I shall include a note, a sarcastic note, on the Bloomsbury baiters. No, I suppose not. Write them down - that's the only way."

However, in 1934, despite Lewis's dislike of homosexuality and the Bloomsbury Group, Spender visited him at 5 Scarsdale Studios. Lewis was very hard up and harassed. There were 3 arm chairs, whisky and glasses on a packing case and candles because there was no electric light. An easel was in the background. Lewis disliked Spender as he was going to be influential in Modern Literature, which is perhaps why he drew Spender. But Spender's support of Lewis and friends was conditional and whilst he admired Campbell's 1936 *Mithraic Emblems* he couldn't write a positive review because Auden was critical of Campbell.

SURVEY OF POETS AND THE SPANISH CIVIL WAR

The contrasting views of the various poets was surveyed in the summer of 1934 when Geoffrey Grigson of *New Verse* sent a short, blunt questionnaire to the poets in whom he was interested, asking them for their opinions on the state of their craft and their political affiliations. Twelve replied, of whom four declared that they were apolitical, two said they were Communists, nobody admitted to being Conservative or Fascist and Lewis found himself "exactly midway between the Bolshevist and the Fascist". Among those who did not reply were Auden, Spender and Day-Lewis.

Day-Lewis was reluctant to nail his colours to the mast as a communist, fearing how it would be viewed by his employers at the school. He wrote in a letter to Grigson: "Yes, I received the copy of the questionnaire: I meant to write and tell you that I would rather not answer it, but I forgot. One or two of the questions I felt quite incapable of answering, and some of the others seemed to me unanswerable in any brief space. Actually several of them are dealt with indirectly in my book, which will be out on September 1st [*A Hope for Poetry*]. I'm asking Blackwell to send you a copy. There are (at least) four printer's errors in it, which will provide the enemy with a good basis for criticism."

Not answering counted against him as Grigson decided that he was a light-weight Auden follower and embarked on a vendetta against him in *New Verse*. Grigson called *A Hope for Poetry* "a bad book" which "Mr Day-Lewis, instead of writing for his equals or his betters, has written to persuade others to read himself, Mr Spender and Mr Auden. An inferior purpose has bred an inferior book, evasive on the poet and politics. ridiculous often in judgement ... and in prose style as cheaply poetical as Mr Humbert Wolfe ... or any other Sunday journal buffoon. There is a nasty resemblance between "*A Hope for Poetry*" and a romance for boys written not long ago by the same writer."

Day-Lewis had contributed a political, poem to the July issue of *New Verse* but by October moved his allegiance to a new, rival, journal, *Left Review*, of the British section of the Communist-run Writers International. Spender was also involved in this journal and both poets provoked Grigson's scorn.

In 1935, Spender supported Day-Lewis's next book *A Time to Dance,* saying that it "contains much the most beautiful poetry you have written" that it showed a new lack of inhibition. However, Spender wasn't blindly partisan in his praise: "In all your early work I find that there is a slight stiffness ... too much emphasis on the stiff upper lip ... which puts me off a good deal, and even annoys me occasionally." And; "often in your work you simply replace what you are really writing about with something else, by a very simple process not of symbolism, but of comparison. For instance in "*In Me Two Worlds*" one almost sees a Punch cartoon with two worlds drawn, one on each side of the, sheet, and with Communism written on one and Capitalism on the other, and with you (labelled Cecil) standing in the middle."

But of his new style "you aren't depraved enough to write like this, you haven't even got a developed and sophisticated enough sense of humour, at least I don't think you have. There are great advantages in being depraved, you know what, one can soak oneself in and emerge from "the destructive element", but you have different standards, that is all. Or that's how I see you."

Auden gave support to the Communists as can be seen in a couple of his main poems of the 1930s *Spain* and *September 1, 1939.* But Auden was now becoming established, being awarded the King's Gold Medal for poetry in 1936 (established by John

Masefield after appointment as Laureate to George V), so his poetry was less revolutionary.

The *Left Review* conducted another survey (unrelated to Grigson's) in 1937, named *Authors Take Sides on the Spanish Civil War*. Nancy Cunard, Auden and Spender helped to distribute it and 127 out of 148 writers replied. T. S. Eliot, Ezra Pound, Virginia Woolf and James Joyce chose to "take no part" or didn't reply and were in the minority. Spender, Day-Lewis and Rebecca West all supported the Republicans.

Day-Lewis said; "Both as a writer and as a member of the Communist Party... I am bound to help in the fight against Fascism, which means certain destruction or living death for humanity." He believed that poetry should have a public and political role. He saw anxious times where others were risking their lives in Spain. "I look upon it quite simply as a battle between light and darkness, of which only a blind man could be unaware."

But whilst he could not remain silent he was becoming less clear about the answer. His faith in a revolution and the creation of a Soviet-style republic in Britain was leaving him.

Ch 19 : *THE ADDICT* (1930 - 1935)

Pamela Frankau, the daughter of the popular novelist Gilbert Frankau, had published her first novel, *Marriage of Harlequin*, in 1927, at the age of eighteen. She lived at 8 Wimpole Street and now travelled to the house of her great-aunt, Mrs Eliza Aria, for luncheon. Aunt Eliza was a literary encourager along the lines of Lady Cunard and was friends with George Moore, Michael Arlen, Osbert Sitwell, Rebecca West and many others. Aunt Eliza admired her great-niece as a modern youth whom she championed.

At the house Frankau met Michael Arlen who wore striped trousers, a black jacket, a double-breasted waistcoat and a thin watch-chain punctuated by pearls.

"Michael," said Aunt Eliza, "this is Pamela. You will probably hate each other."

"Why?" asked Frankau, startled. And Arlen added, "I am sure I shan't hate you."

Frankau removed her hat, and her hair was ruffled. And she was then greeted, briefly, by Mr. Osbert Sitwell.

The room had a long mirror and Chinese curtains. She sat at the foot of the table and Arlen remarked, with amused and friendly eyes, "It is a pity for you to sit with your back to the light." He continued, "I do not like food; I like smoking. These cigarettes are without nicotine, for my health. And this is a new cigarette-case."

"It is a lovely one, Michael," Osbert added with childish applause.

"They say you write like me," said Arlen to Frankau.

They had tea, motzas and butter, ginger biscuits and Goldflake cigarettes from a box with a marble lid. Then they parted, promising to meet again, whilst Aunt Eliza, Osbert and Arlen remained to talk.

"I am in love with him," thought Frankau as she went to a Matinee, heading towards Farringdon Street in a taxi. But he was just a precursor to other relationships.

Later, at Wimpole Street, Frankau met Rebecca West whom Aunt Eliza had said was the cleverest woman in the world. Aunt Eliza, who was enshrined in the room, inspected her and said, "You look very nice. Has any distinguished young man proposed yet?" "Not yet" replied Frankau and Aunt Eliza sighed.

Then West came in, wearing a grey frock patterned with a map of Paris. West was smaller, though fifteen years older than Frankau and with glistening eyes and square shoulders.

They discussed *The Well of Loneliness* (a 1928 lesbian novel by Radclyffe Hall) and Aunt Eliza was unsympathetic, saying; "Such people ought to be put in prison, darling, and that's an end of it."

"I don't want anybody, put in prison," replied West in her light and urgent voice, "Do you?"

Frankau shook her head.

"Have you read it?"

"No," said Frankau, "and I am not going to read it."

"That is an understandably lofty attitude," said West.

And Frankau replied "the abstention actually owes itself to lack of opportunity."

"We must meet again," said West, "though I am headed for Paris and then for America."

Frankau went home quietly impressed and began to worship West's "glamorous, overshadowing personality".

Their friendship developed and in the summer of 1929 West, invited Frankau to come down to the Villa Mysto, an Edwardian villa on an offshore island between Cannes and St Raphael. "My God, do you mean it?" replied Frankau. It was an ideal opportunity to have a five week break and to write her novel.

Shortly after they travelled through France in a hired car with Anthony West who was 15 years old. This was Rebecca West's son from her affair with H.G. Wells (a figure that Frankau saw as "a tired mole with blue eyes and large whiskers."). "The road signposts read like a wine list," said

West as they headed south. "Chablis, Beaune, Nults-St-George, Mersault, Macon."

They travelled through roads sided with red rocks and pine-trees with a hot sun on the blue sea. And came upon the white villa with its ornaments. It was an overwhelmingly female world and "a heaven on earth, with rocks at the bottom of the garden from which one steps into fifteen feet of nicely warmed Mediterranean".

They wore only bathing-suits and cotton trousers. And Frankau listened to West and asked questions like, "Do you believe in God?" from the centre of the swimming-pool. Their skin went scarlet, then blistered and browned. The talk was playful and flirtatious and Frankau laughed until she ached. But was unable to write her novel. West read and praised the work in progress, and Frankau felt "like a Ford being patted on the back by a Hispano-Suiza".

West liked being idolized by someone of the younger generation and described Frankau as being "beautiful in the manner of Disney's Bambi".

Anthony was dazzled by "the beautiful bodies of young women baking in the sun" and was pleased to have an ally in Frankau. They would swim together to small rock-islands and see the octopus staring out at them from the weeds. "I fell head over heels in love with her at fifteen without looking closer", wrote Anthony. She saw that he was unhappy and would listen to him for hours. "The confusions that she helped me with most were about my sexual being. The way I had been brought up had given me the idea that a woman was the thing to be, and that I had somehow done wrong by being a male."

West didn't see this and had thought that the only problem was that she was a working, single mother and wrote in the Daily Mail that autumn, that it puts a strain on society, "When a boy has seen his mother acting as both father and mother, supporting the house as well as managing it, where is he to get his idea of fatherhood?" When he grows up, he may "take it for granted that some woman will do two people's work and father his children as well as mother them".

West wrote about the vacation at Villa Mysto to her sister Lettie: "What it means to send Anthony off to Easton you can guess - it depresses me to death, and of course the way he adores H. G. is ghastly .... The month Anthony was here was a great success. I had Pamela Frankau here and she was an ideal companion for him. She's just 21 but very young for her age:"

Yet West underestimated Frankau's maturity. And Anthony recognised that "Pamela was consciously attempting to mediate between us with a clearer idea of what its (the relationship's) realities were than either I or my mother possessed." Frankau visited Anthony at Stowe public school and took him out to lunch at the nearby "Spread Eagle" pub to talk about the issues that he had with his mother. Frankau supported him and put pressure on West to remove him from Stowe and from psychoanalysis. And this began a lessening of intimacy between her and West.

FRANKAU MEETS HUMBERT

In 1930 West framed a letter from George Moore whom she considered "a moral genius" and her protégé, Frankau, was soon to meet his protégé, Humbert Wolfe. West had had an affair with H.G.Wells, 25 years her elder and her protégé would soon do the same.

In August 1931 Frankau met Humbert at a party given by Viola Garvin of the *Observer* newspaper. She was strikingly good looking and twenty-three years of age. He was a colourful figure of sophistication. But at forty-six Humbert was only two years younger than her father.

Frankau thought that his wit had a "headlong quality" and said that "often he was half-way through an epigram before he saw it coming." Someone at Oxford had said that his eyes often looked astonished at what his mouth had just said. And he could also "look surprised at what his pencil had just written - even if he then decided that it was utterly meaningless and crumpled up the finished product into a ball."

She became besotted and doted on him. But perhaps his real love was poetry.

PORTRAITS OF HUMBERT

In 1928 Humbert was at the peak of his fame as a poet and was at his club when, in his words, the artist Sir William Rothenstein (who, like Wolfe, also originated from Bradford Jewry) "crept in with his drawing board this morning - & made a very good beginning. It's going to be, I think, a real portrait, the first that I have ever had. It will, I fear, be too expensive to buy."

Rothenstein made a series of drawings and studies over the following years and finally, in January 1931, created a portrait of Humbert. It was a peak moment in Humbert's life that was immortalised. And for Humbert it was a final seal of approval from a member of the artistic establishment.

His wife Jessie saw the effect of Rothenstein's portrait on him and she needed another way back into his world. One Sunday afternoon in 1931, sitting at the desk in the library of their flat in Artillery Mansions. Humbert had fallen asleep whilst reading in his big easy chair. The light from the window threw his features into relief. She began to sketch the shadows of his face and when Humbert awoke he was impressed with the strange drawing, though remarked, "it looks like a death-mask." It became one of his bookmarks until it fell out in 1932. She became convinced that she should draw and to paint him, and Wolfe liked the development of her talents. She wanted to capture Humbert's beauty and marvelled that no sculptor, such as Jacob Epstein, had captured his likeness.

She carried a sketch-book and drew him at every opportunity. He encouraged her, sitting in the morning before he left for Whitehall and then later in the day. And sometimes, when he could not keep still, he would say to her, laughing, "You'll have to paint me asleep, or dead."

Meanwhile Humbert had had copies of Rothenstein's picture made and in August 1932 he sent Frankau a copy to her home at 26A Pond Place (near South Kensington Station) and wrote on the back;

"After a year. Pam from Humbert – 31st Aug. '32"

By the end of 1932 Jessie was beginning to suspect him of deceit and accused him of destroying invitations for them both to attend functions. He denied receiving any such invitations. And proposed that they stay in Oxford, where he had been invited to give a lecture." It was there that Albert Rutherston, Rothenstein's brother, Humbert's schooldays friend from Bradford and now Ruskin Master of Drawing, saw her sketch-book and said, with surprise. "But you are really good, Jessie. Come and work with me at the Ruskin." She couldn't leave London but he wrote to the Slade School of Art to introduce her, and she became a student there in 1933. And she worked on her portraits of Humbert, in her studio, every week-end.

WEST MARRIES

For a long time West had been pushed away into the margins of social life for being a single, unmarried parent. She began to want a sort of conventional respectability. So in 1933 she married Henry Andrews and no longer dressed as a shabby bohemian. She wanted to keep their circle to writers despite finding that "The literary world gets fuller and fuller of bitterness." However, West began to give "straight" dinner parties for her husband's business friends at their home in Orchard Court.

Virginia Woolf became irritated with West's "careening society voice" and saw Henry as "such dead, though excellent, mutton". She noted, in her diary, that; "Of course it's admirable in its way - impersonal, breezy, yes, go ahead, facing life, eating dinner at the Savoy, meeting millionaires, woman & man of the worldly; but - no, I must add the kindness intelligence & erudition of the admirable effete spectacled swollen eyed Andrews - the cultivated don turned banker, with his devotion to R. - Cecily he calls her, for whom he buys these fish & bookcases. What's wrong then?"

For Virginia it was "the formality, the social strata they live on – appearances" that was wrong. She felt that West was like Orchard Court itself, "a lit up modern block, floodlit by electricity".

To add to the alienation West was sent malicious letters, by someone who knew her circumstances in detail but chose to remain anonymous. They read like a vulgar parody of Virginia's diaries but could have been from any of a number of rivals;

"With your grandiose ideas you hated your poor father - poor little clerk who was able to afford you only that shabby poverty house on the Edinburgh tramlines, 3 greedy daughters - poor man! You sing well for the supper (Shroder) of the very very odd Henry of the hen-toed walk specks and furtive air your peculiar dud Oxford hubby - no honours degree here, ye gods, no!! Apes well the accent of the "English ruling class" ...."

West clearly had to choose between her old friends like Virginia and her new husband. She signed herself "Cicely Andrews" to Mrs Woolf and they remained acquaintances.

THE ADDICT

In this background when West discovered about her friend and protégé, Pamela Frankau's relationship to Humbert (a married man old enough to be Frankau's father, and about whom all manner of stories circulated in the literary world) West was hurt, jealous and deeply disapproving. She felt that Humbert had 'stolen' Frankau.

She wrote long, furious letters to Frankau and then a 20,000 word short story attacking Humbert. West published *The Addict - Portrait of a man - his loves, his labours and his lies ..* in February 1935, in *Nash's Pall Mall Magazine*. She changed enough details to be safe from a libel action, though was confident he wouldn't bring one as he wouldn't want the scandal as a senior Civil Servant. However he was easily recognisable.

The main character, "Claude Cambray", was a bank employee poet, "addicted" to women, who deceived his wife and girl-friends. He had the good looks of a B-list film star and was dark skinned in appearance. He had a string of women but was also largely impotent. He invented a jealous wife who wouldn't divorce him and lied about his children having died in order to gain sympathy and make him seem like he had suffered like a true Romantic poet.

Frankau said, "She (Rebecca) represented Humbert as dirty, unpopular, stingy, greedy, and wholly without talent: a liar, a sponger, a noceur somewhat handicapped by impotence, a painstaking deceiver of his good simple wife and all his girl friends ... one of whom was me."

In the story Frankau was "Agatha" and Viola Garvin was also there as "Valerie" as Garvin was widely believed to be in love with Humbert, though her feelings were not necessarily reciprocated. West told Frankau about the story just days before publication, saying that it was meant to be funny, and that as Humbert had no shortage of female admirers so the story was nothing new.

Frankau then told her, that although Humbert had a daughter, Ann, the death of his two babies were his cruellest memories. So accusing him of lying about the tragic death of his children was completely false. West was devastated and swore she never knew, but said it was too late to change the story as it was about to be published. She asked Frankau to show Humbert the piece. Frankau said that would not be necessary for West's story was sure of an appreciative readership of "friends" who could be relied upon to do that.

When Frankau told Humbert about the story he sat like a stunned child, worried by the wide circulation that the story immediately received. He didn't lose his temper and judged that his best defence was to disregard the insult. Frankau broke friends with West and wanted to write against her but that saddened Humbert who quoted scripture; "vengeance is mine saith the Lord."

The story gave rise to a small literary explosion, in which that world revelled. His reputation was damaged and it allowed Edith Sitwell to announce confidently that Humbert was one of the geniuses that she had seen come and go. Yet his wife Jessie remained unaware of the furore surrounding her husband and the story seems never to have reached her.

Humbert's absent-mindedness allowed him to quickly get over the episode, however, Frankau bore a grudge for years and eventually wrote a novel called *The Devil We Know*, in which West was maliciously portrayed and would have been even more savage if Humbert hadn't managed to persuade her to tone it down.

In March 1935, Humbert and Jessie celebrated their 25th wedding anniversary. At which he toasted "These have been good years. Here's to the next twenty-five." But the following day he introduced Frankau to Jessie at their home, a flat at 128 Mount Street, Mayfair. Frankau was invited to make up the numbers for a small dinner party and Jessie's first impression of her was as a "sleek-haired, black-eyed young woman with a husky voice". Frankau was a good-looking young woman and it was not long before Jessie began painting her. She would come to the house, with its view across to the Houses of Parliament and Westminster Cathedral, to sit for her portrait. Jessie painted wearing a stylish artist's white coat, with decorative piping on the pockets and lapels, and the painting progressed slowly. She had no idea that when Humbert said he would be at late sittings in the House, or meetings at the Air Ministry, he and Frankau were frequenting London's most fashionable clubs.

Jessie's musings were interrupted in February 1936, after finishing the portrait, by a telephone call from which she learned, for the first time, of Humbert's affair. Frankau was summoned to the house. And there she admitted to having been Humbert's mistress for four years and was then forbidden from the house.

For Jessie all the mysterious events and crises of the past few years, Frankau's sudden entry into their lives and Humbert's late nights were illuminated with all the fearful clarity of a lightning flash. She knew that he had had lovers but never suspected that someone invited into their home would betray them in such a way.

She wanted to avenge herself of all this deceit and sue for divorce but realised that whilst divorce would punish Frankau and any other women with whom Humbert had misbehaved it would also utterly destroy him and make things impossibly difficult for their daughter Ann.

Yet when she confronted Humbert that evening he told her that he must live as he pleased and showed no sign of responsibility for the upheaval. So she left the house to stay with her sister for the night, saying that she would go to Oxford the next day to see their daughter.

She returned the next morning to pick up some clothes, she found a letter which Humbert had left blaming the "blackmailers" and saying: "The question is whether you will immediately disorganize the structure you have patiently built, or whether you will take a little time for reflection." It concluded that he would be staying at his club, The Athenaeum, and would return home whenever she asked him to do so.

Jessie considered her situation and came to blame all the women who had tried to "collect" her husband, more than Humbert. She thought that he had as many sides to his personality as a Harlequin's dress, and each woman matched just one of these Harlequin colours. And so she decided not to give up her husband, daughter and home, without a fight.

But whilst he had reasons why he didn't want their marriage to end he would not agree to any limitation on his actions. And his replies to her letters had all the evasions of a Civil Servant determined not to answer awkward questions.

Ch 20 : LAWRENCE OF ARABIA (1919 - 1935)

Throughout these times a key person in sanctioning the work of poets was the semi-legendary T.E. Lawrence. This ascetic figure of immense vitality was known as "Lawrence of Arabia" and his war memoirs were *The Seven Pillars of Wisdom*. These were his way to exorcise the terrible memories of battle in an account of his leadership of the Arab Revolt in the desert, with himself as both intellectual and boys' adventure hero.

Lawrence changed from a pre-1914 academic archaeologist into a guerrilla leader in the campaign against the Turks in the Middle East. He became a proponent of Arab self-determination (which was betrayed by the Treaty of Versailles).

In 1919 Lawrence was 31 years old and returned to his life as an Oxford archaeologist and a Fellow of All Souls. His friendships had a hypnotic sense of mystical understanding. However, he was also emotionally and physically awkward and hated being touched. Despite this poets found him influential and inspiring.

GRAVES AND LAWRENCE

Robert Graves met him in 1919 and showed him his poems. Lawrence made suggestions that he accepted for his *The Pier-Glass* (1921), a volume that he dedicated to Lawrence. They would remain close friends and Graves was one of the few people with whom Lawrence discussed his masochistic homosexual experiences.

In 1921 Graves had recurring bouts of shell shock and was haunted by war memories. He felt guilty for the men who died under his command and was close to a breakdown. A nerve specialist told him to stop working and to put off taking his final examinations until the following year. So Graves left Oxford without a degree (although ways were found to enrol him for a B Litt thesis). He earned very little from writing and when his grant ended all he had was a small war pension to support himself, his wife and children on. Sir Walter Raleigh,

Head of the School of English, wanted to help and arranged for his appointment as Professor of English at Sandhurst, but Graves turned down the offer to his father's astonishment.

He and his wife were near to being declared bankrupt yet both seemed to be indifferent to the fact. Her father sent some money, however, Graves began to blame his troubles on his muse Nancy, seeing her as an impractical idealist who was too young, not seductive and not the right person.

Graves' work as a poet and critic progressed despite these financial difficulties and his thesis for the B Litt, was good enough to be published before it was examined in 1926. In 1925 Graves was appointed as the first Professor of English at the new University of Cairo. The appointment required influence as he lacked qualifications and was emotionally unstable. The role sounded good, as it had only two lectures a week, and Graves had relatives in Egypt. His half-brother Richard was a diplomat there and his half-sister Molly lived in Cairo.

Graves and Nancy invited the writer Laura Riding to come to England and then accompany them to Egypt. Despite any previous difficulties with him Siegfried Sassoon was also invited to accompany them to Egypt, but declined, buying them a car instead and sending it from England. However, Edith Sitwell was upset because Graves left without saying goodbye.

Once there Graves hated Egypt and the job. The children became ill, Nancy missed England and Riding became bored and had hysterical temper-tantrums - becoming so excited that she fainted. He also upset the British community as he would attend university events with Riding instead of Nancy.

So he resigned before his first year was over and they returned to England where Riding was his lover. Nancy and the children stayed in the country in her father's house in Cumberland, painting and designing dresses. And Graves and Riding settled in Ladbroke Square in London.

Financial problems led Graves to sell the car. Then Lawrence helped, giving them a first edition of *The Seven Pillars of Wisdom* which sold for £330.96. And when Lawrence no longer wanted his shortened version of *The Seven Pillars of*

Wisdom kept in print, Graves was allowed to write and publish a short book on the topic, called *Lawrence and the Arabs* (1927). Graves received an advance of £500 and it sold well, remaining in print for many years. Lawrence sent Graves manuscripts and signed copies of books, which he could sell, and also recommended Graves to producers and directors needing a scriptwriter. And although Graves would earn large sums of money it quickly disappeared with only a small amount being used to buy an old printing press to start his own publishing house, the Seizin Press.

Riding and Graves formed a magic Circle that practiced astrology and sexual four-somes. Nancy was progressive and used to cycle to Oxfordshire villages to explain to women about how to use contraception when it was still illegal. She was part of the circle and this was the stuff of the London newspaper gossip columns. On the evening of 26 April 1929 Riding claimed that the fourth member, Geoffrey Taylor, had mistreated her and the Circle. He refused to apologize and the argument continued the next morning. Riding went out of the room and returned saying that she had drunk poison, Lysol. It had no effect so she shouted "Goodbye, chaps" and jumped out of a third floor window. Graves ran down the staircase and jumped after her from a window a half storey lower.

Riding was hospitalized for months with a broken pelvis, a bent spinal cord, and four crushed lumbar vertebrae. Graves blamed himself. Geoffrey was jealous of Graves and reported the matter the police, who interviewed Graves on suspicion of attempted murder. He was cleared in the investigation but wouldn't say that Riding had jumped as attempted suicide was a crime that would mean that Riding would be deported back to America so Graves used his contacts to prevent her prosecution.

Meanwhile Geoffrey and Nancy (who now lived together on a barge with the children) suggested renewing the Holy Circle but Graves wanted Riding to himself and rejected the proposal. He wrote to Nancy saying that "I love Laura beyond everything thinkable and that has always been so". And he told Nancy "The children are yours".

Graves did what he could to prevent Geoffrey from finding employment. And only a court order forced him to return Geoffrey's books. He also sent a bill demanding payment for the clothes he had given Geoffrey after Riding burnt his possessions during an initiation ritual.

And Graves' personal life didn't get any less complicated. By 1931 he had a German mistress whom he made pregnant and Riding forced them to have an abortion. But Graves and T.E. Lawrence remained friends despite their sexual differences. By now Graves rejected his homosexuality and believed that single-sex schools create homosexuality which was tolerated at universities. Perhaps their bond remained because both disliked Modernist poetry and mass democracy and both were elitists seeking a primal spiritual renewal.

They were such good friends that when, shortly before his death in 1935, Lawrence had a foreboding he would die Graves prepared an obituary with his help. He chose Graves because he thought that Graves would write what he wanted.

LEWIS AND LAWRENCE

Another war scarred writer, Wyndham Lewis, was friends with Lawrence. Both were soldiers who had demonstrated their courage under fire. And both were multi-talented and self-declared outsiders who covered their vulnerable core with a show of aggression. And in their conflicting desires for obscurity and publicity, they were both extreme eccentrics.

After returning to Oxford Lawrence enlisted in the lower ranks of the Tank Corps under a pseudonym, to avoid the lime-light. He was damaged from the war and needed help. In October 1922 Lawrence told his and Lewis' mutual friend, Sir William Rothenstein, that he would like Lewis to illustrate a lavish and privately printed edition of *Seven Pillars of Wisdom*.

In 1924 Lawrence sped into London on his powerful motorcycle, scaled the garden wall around Lewis' studio in Holland Park and suddenly appeared out of the night. Lewis, always on guard, mistook him for a tradesman's bully. And after

Lewis realised his mistake Lawrence asked him to read his still unpublished *Seven Pillars of Wisdom*.

Lewis read the work and described the character and behaviour of Lawrence as of a "meta-physical boy-scout". He questioned Lawrence about his motives for enlisting again after the end of the war and saying farewell to ambition. Lawrence's replied: "I was an Irish nobody. I did something. It was a failure. And I became an Irish nobody again". Lewis was unconvinced by the explanation as Lawrence had written to Graves that he had re-enlisted under various names to try and avoid the public limelight as ways to avoid women. And Lewis did not like homosexuality. Nevertheless, Lewis was depressed by "the spectacle of this stupid waste of so much ability."

He asked why Lawrence had refused the offer to be Governor of Egypt, and Lawrence replied that "if he had to sit in judgement on another man, he would always feel that he should be where the accused man was."

Lewis believed that the political powers "got the better of him, and his Arab friends suffered at the same time a disillusion." He believed that Lawrence "acted very nobly in refusing to participate in a political fraud." However, he thought that Lawrence was "far too intelligent ever to imagine that the war would result in the ideal emergence of a powerful and independent Arabian State."

Despite their conversations and friendship Lewis didn't complete the drawings until too late as he was working on his own major books. And although Lawrence admired Lewis' art he did not admire his writing.

SASSOON & LAWRENCE

Lawrence had friendly corresponded with Noel Coward for a while and Coward had teased him over his wish for anonymity, writing; "Dear 338171, or may I call you 338?" Lawrence concluded that Coward was "not deep but remarkable. A hasty kind of genius."

A deeper friend was Siegfried Sassoon and Lawrence had first wanted to meet Sassoon after reading his *Counter-Attack* (1918). Although both had been heroic soldiers Lawrence recognised something of extreme recklessness in Sassoon. And even Lawrence, a lover of powerful motorcycles, was fearful after 5 minutes of being driven in "Mad Jack's" car.

Then one evening in 1923 Sassoon was at home in Tufton Street, lighting the fire, when the doorbell rang. He answered the door and was surprised to find Lawrence standing in the porch in a new soft grey hat. Sassoon saw him as "a little man in a long, ready-made-looking, rough brown "ulster"" with a large brown paper parcel under his arm.

"I've been craving to talk to you for weeks," said Sassoon.

Lawrence replied, "I'm on leave from the army to see General Trenchard about transferring back to the RAF. I want to discuss Seven Pillars."

Lawrence wanted him to read *The Seven Pillars Of Wisdom* before it was published for the public. And Sassoon said, "I feel overwhelmed by the honour". Despite feeling enormous besides his small, self-contained visitor. Sassoon blundered about the room, blurting out questions and assertions, about Lawrence's book, his health and his prospects. Then Sassoon exclaimed to the quiet Lawrence "What I can't understand is how you came to be a Colonel." Lawrence felt charmed by the question.

Sassoon read the manuscript and felt as though he had lived through an epic. And by November 1923 Sassoon was enthralled by Lawrence's charismatic power and thought that Lawrence's aura was especially strong. He saw Lawrence as an "Infallible superman" but felt protective towards him as Lawrence drank tea and nibbled shortbread and sponge cakes.

"Is any of it worthwhile?" asked Lawrence.

Sassoon replied, "Damn you, how long do you expect me to go on reassuring you about your bloody masterpiece. It is a GREAT BOOK, blast you. Are you satisfied? You tank-investigating eremite."

"That's wonderful," said Lawrence. "Only judgments like yours can give me any rest on this point. It means a lot."

And in 1926 Sassoon shared T.E.'s *Seven Pillars of Wisdom* manuscript (Sassoon called Lawrence "T.E.") with the influential Sir Edmund Gosse .

And the admiration was reciprocal, Sassoon's prose debut in 1928 *Memoirs of a Fox-Hunting Man* has an Englishness that Lawrence admired. As well as sharing likes they shared dislikes and in 1931 Lawrence requested extra copies of *Poems of Pinchbeck Lyre* (the book attacking Humbert Wolfe). Their friendship also caused consternation in Sassoon's other relationships. Whilst on holiday with Stephen Tennant in Syracuse in 1930 as Tennant painted flowers and admired shells he wondered, to Sassoon, why Lawrence hadn't submitted to the Turkish boy who made homosexual advances at him (as described in *The Seven Pillars of Wisdom*). Sassoon raged at Tennant and criticised his "bottle party standards of morality". Tennant wept before the usual reconciliation. But this, along with Tennant's attitudes towards Hardy, added to the tension in their relationship, ending with Tennant leaving him in 1933.

Lawrence's importance to Sassoon was spiritual and not sexual. Lawrence had visited Sassoon after Sassoon had a bout of shingles and was worried that he might lose his sight. Lawrence gave an act of healing and he recovered.

And in the early 1930s Lawrence invited Sassoon to tea at his cottage in Dorset. Lawrence was in his army mechanic's uniform and Sassoon saw him as a "queer little figure in dark motor-overalls, his brown and grimy face framed in a fur-lined cap." Sassoon was interested in Lawrence's relationship to another guest "Little Russell", Lawrence was serving under the pseudonym "Private Shaw" at Southampton and made friends with the instructor, a lance-corporal. Sassoon thought that he was Lawrence's male lover but Lawrence was too discreet for him to be sure. It was many years before Lawrence's prediliction for being flogged, sparked off by his rape in the war, became public knowledge. But even though Sassoon didn't know about this he was still disapproving as he was snobbish and his lovers tended to be aristocratic or upper-middle-class, conspicuously "pretty" and a lot younger than himself.

By 1933 Sassoon was on good terms with Edith again, persuading the Royal Society of Literature to award her the A.C. Benson Silver Medal for Poetry. And when, in 1934, Sassoon became engaged. Edith told Sassoon that she was "thrilled and delighted at his engagement" to Hester but then told her sister-in-law "I suppose the bridal pair will want to adopt ST (Stephen Tennant)".

Lawrence was worried that "marriage would conventionalize Sassoon and doubted that the marriage would survive. Though he found Hester charming he saw her as a "foolhardy creature for taking on" Sassoon.

Sassoon married Hester Gatty in 1934 and Lawrence came to the wedding on his motorcycle called "Boaneges" and Hester adored him. But Stephen Tennant burst into tears on hearing about the wedding.

In July 1934 Lawrence visited them in their huge house which was furnished in Mansion style. Sassoon was abnormally happy and full of jest. Lawrence found Sassoon's new verses *Vigils* "exquisite chiselled" and the balancing verses of Sassoon "deserve to be read almost as minutely as they were made. What an iconic stillness there is about his images now. He has progressed from flesh and blood to bronze."

Lawrence was also friends with the Sitwells and possessed a brass head of Osbert by the sculptor Frank Dobson. But the friendship was never as great at those towards Graves and Sassoon.

LAWRENCE SUPPORTS DAY-LEWIS

Despite Lawrence's support and friendship of ex-soldiers Graves and Sassoon he favoured another poet as his new light. This poet shared Sassoon's appreciation of Hardy's subjectivity and the suffering individual despite T.S. Eliot's making those approaches unfashionable. Hardy was attacked in 1934 by Eliot in *After Strange Gods; A Primer of Modern Heresy*;

"He [Hardy] seems to me to have written as nearly for the sake of "self-expression" as a man well can; and the self which he had to express does not strike me as a particularly wholesome or edifying matter of communication."

However, instead of Sassoon coming to the defence it was the young Cecil Day-Lewis who championed Hardy. He criticized Eliot for writing impersonal poetry with no human personality, saying "that he achieves poetry only by excluding large areas of personal experience." By contrast "Hardy put everything he felt, everything he noticed, everything he was into his poetry. As a result he wrote a great many bad poems - far more than Mr Eliot ever wrote - [but] his poetry has that breadth of matter and manner which only a major poet can compass."

Day-Lewis wanted poetry to engage with the world in crisis and his own personal *Transitional Poem*, published by the Woolf's Hogarth Press in 1929, had been a breakthrough to critical acclaim. It was the first major poem of the revolution of the poets of the 1930s. However, the good start stalled. It was not until his 1934 *The Magnetic Mountain* that he would continue his progress. Initially it didn't receive much attention or acclaim. It was published by the Hogarth Press and even when it received critical acclaim they had 144 copies of the original print-run of 500 piled up, covered with a cloth and used as seats until a year after publication. And then there was a sudden demand for copies.

The boost came from Lawrence, when on August 15, 1934, the *London Evening Standard* published an article in the gossip columns titled *England's Great Man*.

"Recently Mr Winston Churchill and Colonel T.E. (Aircraftman Shaw) Lawrence met at the country house of a British Minister. The two men had a discussion in which present company was excepted, on the dearth of great men in the post-war period. Mr Churchill scouted the idea that there were any great men in England at the present moment.

Aircraftman (Colonel T.E. Lawrence) Shaw was more optimistic. He claimed that he had discovered one great man in these islands. His name is Cecil Day-Lewis. He was, of course, unknown to the other guests...

Mr Lewis's claim to greatness is based on his poetry. He has four volumes of verse to his credit. Here is a sample:

"Farewell again to this adolescent moon;
I say it is a bottle
For hapless poets to feed their fancy on.
Once mine sucked there, and I dreamed
The heart a record for the gramophone."

When he is not writing poetry, Mr Lewis is a schoolmaster."

The article began a friendship between Lawrence and Day-Lewis (despite the quotation from *Transitional Poem* incorrectly reading "hapless" instead of "papless") and started a run on his volumes at Hogarth Press. It put Day-Lewis' name in the public consciousness and his image as a good-looking public schoolmaster with a wife and small child made him appear unthreatening at a time when Europe's political future was full of threats. He presented a more acceptable image for the leader of a new English literary movement, than W.H. Auden or Stephen Spender, who were indulging themselves in Berlin.

However, the description of Day-Lewis as a great Englishman was noted as a black mark against him in the school where he worked. "Lawrence apparently told Winston Churchill that I was the one great man in England, which was rather hard on poor We," Day-Lewis wrote to Spender, "& in consequence my name is as much mud to the common room as it is to Grigson's *"New Verse"*."

Despite Lawrence's praise he wrote to Day-Lewis from the Ozone Hotel in Bridlington to complain that Day-Lewis's next book, *A Hope for Poetry*, was "only half an effort". Lawrence thought it was "only half an argument". "So long as you wrote poems I was content with reading them, Over Dick Willoughby I laughed, This, as I say; is different." Lawrence wanted the new generation to break links with their past but this rejected a central claim of "*A Hope for Poetry*". He didn't like Day-Lewis's concentration on "those few thought-ridden poets" like Donne and was "glad" when Day-Lewis instead "concentrated on Auden, Spender and yourself."

Lawrence predicted "Auden makes me fear that he will not write much more. Spender might, on the other hand, write too much. You have given numbers of us the greatest pleasure - though for me "*The Magnetic Mountain*" was a qualified pleasure." He warned "Poets hope too much, and their politics, like their sciences, usually stink after 20 years."

Then Lawrence wrote to Day-Lewis on 20 December, saying that after all *A Hope for Poetry* "isn't a bad book at all". And on Day-Lewis's next book *A Time to Dance* Lawrence wrote, "I shall enjoy buying your book, so please don't send it - after all, you don't write so many as all that!"

5 months after writing the letter, on the 14th May 1935, Lawrence crashed on his Brough Superior SS100 motorcycle in Dorset, trying to avoid an errand boy on a bicycle.

LAWRENCE'S DEATH

On the 17th May Sassoon learned about the motorcycle crash. It seemed that Lawrence might survive but on the 19th he died after being unconscious for five days. When Sassoon heard of his death he couldn't speak of the tragedy to his wife Hester and just stomped out of the room.

That night he had a flood of reassurance as he felt a hand touch his head. He told Hester about this on the way to the funeral. She had felt the same and both believed that they had been visited by Lawrence.

The funeral was held in a village church in Moreton in Dorset, near Lawrence's home at Clouds Hill. The mourners included Winston Churchill, who cried besides the grave. And Sassoon rebuked 3 photographers as he didn't want it to be a media circus like Hardy's funeral had been.

Sassoon would long for Lawrence to return from the dead to "illuminate the nocturnal landscape" for him. But again his dedicatory poem about a poet that he loved and respected, this time Lawrence not Hardy, was to be rejected by *The Times*;

> "Behold I show you a mystery.
> when I received that sign
> in the dawn of the day which followed the day when you died,
> then was belief made mine;
> for a spirit was with me; a presence was there at my side."

Ch 21 : HITLER - *TRUFFLE EATER* (1933-1936)

In the 1930s Humbert Wolfe and his lover Pamela Frankau entertained many literary figures including Victor Gollancz and his wife, Ruth, Frankau's actress friend Margaretta Scott and Kate Maugham (daughter of Somerset Maugham). Kate was "the only real rival to Frankau in Humbert's wide affections" as he was very fond of her and she was equally fond of him. And Robin Maugham made friends with Humbert through Kate about the time that he went up to Trinity Hall, Cambridge in 1934.

Humbert liked the admiration of friends who were of Frankau's age group. They were young, good looking and thoroughly upper-middle class. They spoke in clipped English and had just the right amount of intelligence, enthusiasm and humour. But when he stayed at Tye House, the Maughams' country house near Heathfield, he nearly collapsed from exhaustion from the physical games they played.

Robin wrote that; "Humbert was one of the cleverest men I've ever met. While staying with us at Tye he would take up the Times and complete the crossword puzzle within five minutes and I didn't believe those who said he could accomplish this feat only because he set the puzzles himself. He was also splendidly witty. I will give only one example. Leon M. Lion, the impresario, was leaving Kate's house after a cocktail party. Leon was extremely courtly in a pompous, old-fashioned way; he was also very fond of drink. At the door, he inclined himself in a dignified manner and kissed Kate's hand.

"Gracious lady, "he mumbled, "never have I enjoyed a cocktail so much."

"What you mean," said Humbert who was standing by, "is that you have never enjoyed a cocktail so often."

And Humbert used to make light fun of Robin's fiancee, Gill Dearmer, by introducing her as "the daughter of a Canon of Westminster who doesn't believe in God". Humbert seemed "terribly old" to her with his grizzled hair but remembered his "immense kindness to us young ones - he was interested in what we were up to." She told Humbert that at a dinner-party she had met Harold Nicolson to which he replied "I wish he had been eaten by an elephant". She was surprised, unaware that Nicolson had written a dismissive review of his *The Uncelestial City.*

Gollancz was closer to Humbert's age and helped Humbert after he became more marginalised (though still a household name that could help sell anthologies). And when Humbert got together with Gollancz at dinner parties in the 1930s, they would tell Jewish stories, in Jewish accents, with an enthusiasm that left their audience hysterical:

"What sort of composer was Mozart?"

"Mozart? Mozart? Rotten! Why, he wrote Faust."

"No, he didn't."

"What, he didn't even write Faust? Didn't I say he was a rotten composer?"

However, Gollancz's downside was that he revelled in open dalliances, taking Humbert's close friend Viola Garvin on "holiday". And he also embarrassed Frankau by making advances towards her in a taxi and when she rebuffed him he took refuge in "You do love my Ruthie, don't you?"

But both men lived for politics and literature. And after having retreated from poetry for a while Humbert began to see a purpose for satire. He had seen the changes when he visited Germany in the summer of 1930 and identified the threat which Nazism posed to peace, the Jewish people and to Christian values. So, in 1933, he published *The Truffle Eater* a book of illustrated poetry that attacked Hitler and the Nazis when few others spoke out against them. And Humbert took a pseudonym Oistros (Greek for a gadfly) to protect his Whitehall career.

> *Shock-Troop Headed Adolf*
> "Look at Adolf where he stands
> With his Nazi hair and hands,
> Murmuring beneath his breath
> Like the lady of Macbeth,
> As he seeks in vain to blot,
> What he sees : "Out damned spot."

And from *The Story of Goering who would not have the Jews*
"Kind Mama, discreetly purring,
Thus addresses bully Goering :
"Child, in the all seeing plan
For the chosen Aryan,
Jews exist to give the Teuton
Something he can wipe his boot on..."

Then in 1934 Humbert began *X at Oberamergau* whilst on holiday in Briancon with Frankau. The long poem is about a 10 yearly German festival of the Passion of Christ. In Humbert's version Christ Himself arrives to play himself and ends up being crucified. In the poem the actor who should have played Christ falls ill and a wandering stranger, X, comes to the town and takes his place. Mary the Mother, Mary Magdalen and the disciple John accept the stranger but the Nazi State Commissioner, Herr Hans "Kanalgeruch" (sewer-stench), suspects that he is a Jew. Kanalgeruch and X's fellow-actors, led by Judas, then crucify the stranger for real. Kanalgeruch:

"Gangster by choice, storm-trooper, and then putscher,
his civic occupation as pork-butcher,
made it seem more than probable that he might
have been designed as Nature's Anti-Semite
by God and by His first pan-German Bishop
to visit Oberammergau and dish up
a Passion-Play purged of the ugly libel
that the Jews had some connection with the Bible."

However the stranger survives in the Resurrection;

"He has gone down to death. Cease, women, your sorrow.
There is nothing for you to lament and naught to cry on.
He has taken death under his arm like an arrow
whose barb is broken. Lift up your gates, O Zion ...."

X at Oberammergau, was published in 1935 by Methuen and the politics of the time were so contentious that it carried a disclaimer that the poem was not "a criticism of a political system or of any person connected with that system"

Despite Humbert's problems from Rebecca West's attacks at the time the reviewers found the poem impressive, however, Christianity was no longer fashionable in contemporary poetry.

And following his marital problems Humbert took a flat in 1936 at 75 Eccleston Square, near Victoria Station. And at this time he was in the Ministry of Labour and in a position to help refugees get out of Hitler's way.

When H. G. Wells retired from the Chairmanship of the international P.E.N. Club (Poets, Playwrights, Essayists, Editors and Novelists) in 1936 Humbert took over Wells' other role as British member of the Executive of P.E.N. The society had been started in England to encourage the interchange of literature and to support writers who suffered hardship.

So members of the PEN club would meet to work to get Jewish writers out of Hitler's Regime. Humbert repatriated people of many artistic branches. This included architects into the offices of Clough Williams-Ellis (designer of the Portmeirion Village in Wales) who wrote that:

"Humbert was in a position to help some of those who had to get out of Hitler's way – and help them he did most devotedly, incidentally landing me in due course with a couple of Austrian architects for whom I had to try and find face-saving work of some sort in my already war-shadowed and overstaffed office."

Humbert also helped on a more political level. That year there was to be a P.E.N. Congress in Rome at which Wells had believed that P.E.N. could take a stand against fascism. Humbert knew that this would flatter the fascists by giving them undue attention. The French agreed with Humbert and so the stand against fascism was put into general principles so that the fascists were not able to engage in prestige seeking grandstanding.

During this time Humbert's wife Jessie stayed on with his daughter Ann in Mount Street. Payment of her allowance was becoming more and more irregular. Her lawyer did all he could to get Humbert to make regular payments, but his income would not pay for two establishments, foreign travel, entertaining his friends at The Berkeley, The Ivy and The Savoy. So she threatened divorce which he did not want because it would cost him his inheritance from his father. He replied that he would resign from the Civil Service, thus leaving them all penniless.

However, she was still paying off a loan that she had raised for him in 1934, and in return for him taking over a loan she consented to sign a Private Deed of Separation in August 1938, hoping that they could tear it up before too long.

Despite the bitterness he still had concern for their safety and at the news of the Munich crisis (the Nazis annexing parts of Czechoslovakia) in September Jessie received a message from Humbert that she and Ann should go to live in Dorset. This concern touched her but they were determined to stay and take up A.R.P. (Air Raid Precautions) work.

The outrage at Munich led to over half a million civilians enrolling in the A.R.P. A Central Register was created within the Ministry of Labour to record the names and qualifications of the applicants. Humbert also helped draw up a list of writers, artists and archaeologists whose services could be employed.

Humbert's friend Albert Rutherston, who was Head of Ruskin College, Oxford also sent him a letter. He had collected a list of writers and artists who wanted to help with the war effort. Humbert thanked him for the list which was added to the Whitehall list.

Denys Kilham Roberts, the secretary of the Society of Authors, Playwrights and Composers also wrote to Humbert suggesting that a committee of authors would be useful in wartime propaganda campaigns. Humbert agreed that authors had a contribution to make but said "I cannot feel that the appointment of a Committee of Authors would not lead to anything but continuous bickering and would not be of real help to the Department. After many years experience in working on committees with authors, I have found them, apart from their special gifts, extraordinarily ignorant and ill-informed people on most topics. The reason for this is the obvious one; that their contacts with the outside world are often limited and that they tend to live in a small and separate universe."

At this time Humbert was Principal Assistant Secretary and Deputy Secretary Designate in the Ministry of Labour and was busy organising the deployment of man-power in preparation for a Second World War. He greeted people with a jovial, "How does it march?" but the strain was showing in his strong, bony and now almost haggard face.

By October 1938 the Manpower Committee thought that the Ministry of Labour should produce and distribute a Handbook on National Service to "explain what types of people were wanted for particular services..." Various Departments contributed and Humbert edited it. Then, in January 1939, the Handbook was distributed to every household in the country. This led to Humbert's boast that he was the only living author whose first edition had run to twenty-million copies.

He got all the young British members of P.E.N. to sign up for voluntary services such as distributing gas masks, the army etc and they all joined up to send the numbers up and to give Humbert something to rattle at the Germans.

In 1938 Robin Maugham had discussed with Humbert the possibility of national service work. And by April 1939 Humbert arranged for him to become private secretary to Sir Herbert Morgan who had just been appointed Director of the National Service Campaign.

And Humbert helped with other appointments. In March 1939, after the 7th Annual P.E.N. dinner at the Savoy, the writer Margaret Storm Jameson, Pamela Frankau, Vera Brittain and others went to Humbert's flat in Eccleston Square. Frankau was doing the honours but their affair was not universally known and Brittain couldn't work out if she lived there or just visited. Humbert showed Brittain a photo of Viola Garvin and told her that Garvin's lameness resulted from the removal of her knee-cap muscles as a child. He also showed them all his review books with autographed letters in them. Storm Jameson and Brittain didn't get home until 1am. Shortly afterwards Storm Jameson was offered the position of president of P.E.N. following the advice of Humbert who wrote "I have found her very clear-minded, sensible and unemotional. She stands deservedly high in the literary world and does not belong to any particular faction."

And whilst this all transpired Humbert continued his own literary work. In 1939 his next book of verse, *Out of Great Tribulation* was published by Gollancz. He called it a baring of the throat to the critics. And despite all the attacks on him he now fully returned to his love of poetry and satire. One key poem was *Turn again Dick Whittington (Theme with variations: A Contribution to Modern Technology)* which sends up Eliot's requirement of the reader to understand his many "learned" allusions -

> "Valiantly the spectres gibber,
> poor rats behind the arras -
> Polonii clenching the stuff in
> dead men's teeth - but they only embarrass
> the dignity of Styx - the oldest man ribber
> that keeps on rollin' for ever and says nuffin' .
> Because there is nuffin' to say?
> Or because there is too much to impart ...
> and the news of the day
> is the blood of the journalist.
> As the blood of Viscount Rothermere
> is the seed of the Press .."

The poem ends with the Note – "For the better comprehension of this poem readers are recommended to begin by mastering all the volumes in the British Museum. A knowledge of Middle Aramaic, though not indispensible, will be helpful."

And Humbert was also happy to make forays into hostile literary territory. Wyndham Lewis wrote in 1939 that; "not long before Humbert Wolfe's death I met him at dinner, and Wolfe observed: "I admire what you write. I do not *like* it." That was a highly civilized remark. A saying that is perhaps the most famous illustration of that type of mature intelligence is Voltaire's – "I detest what you say, but I would defend with my life your right to say it.""

Lewis found little of worth in Humbert and compared him, unfavourably, to T.S.Eliot and James Joyce; "I became an artist and an "intellectual": yet that should only be done today if you have private means, or of course after you have taken a job. Should you, however, take a job, it occupies too much of your time. As an "intellectual" you deteriorate. So it resolves itself, as a rule, into money, or no intellectuality. This statement must be qualified to except the poet. A poem is usually a small short piece of work. It doesn't take long to write "My love is like a red red rose". For the rest of the day you can be a clerk, or an immigration official like the late Humbert Wolfe, or, for that matter a milk-roundsman or window-cleaner. Mr. T. S. Eliot worked originally in a city bank. - He took a job almost at once. A more agreeable and lucrative one was speedily found for him than bank-clerking. He became a working partner in what was at that time a new firm of publishers. That - if the job is not a very exacting one - is about the best thing a poet can do, who has no fortune...James Joyce, for instance. To that penniless language-teacher a strange accident happened. A Quaker lady, Miss Harriet Weaver, at the psychological moment, made him the present of an adequate income, putting down a capital sum to be used in that way, so that he could live thereafter in peace and do his work. It was therefore as a rentier that he wrote *"Ulysses"* and *"Finnegans Wake"*. With emotion Joyce told me, while engaged upon *"Ulysses"*, that he, his wife, and his children would have been on the streets had it not been for this benefactress, unknown personally to him."

However, despite the dismissive comment, Humbert & Pamela Frankau agreed with Lewis on the principle of this matter as in September 1939 they had themselves thought that it seemed highly unlikely, as well as slightly indecent, to think of earning a living as a writer. But this was Humbert's strength, that he could both work and write at a high level.

On January 5th 1940, after the outbreak of war, Humbert died from overwork. Whilst Virginia Woolf wrote scathingly of him in her diary the following day 200 attended his funeral at St-Martins-in-the-Field at Trafalgar Square. Jessie, who was still his wife and still loved him, drew and painted him whilst he lay in state. He was buried under a Hawthorn Tree at Kensal Green Cemetery, in keeping with one of his poems from 1924.

HAWTHORN-TREE

When I am old,
and need a crutch,
and nothing I do
pleases me much,

I'll go and sit
where I can see
spring sunlight on
a hawthorn-tree.

And if that leaves me
cold, I'll have
hawthorn planted
on my grave.

CH 22: THE LEFT BOOK CLUB (1936 – 1938)

The publisher Victor Gollancz followed a very different political path to Humbert Wolfe. In 1936 Gollancz set up the *Left Book Club* as an "educational body" with the goals of the preservation of peace, the creation of a just society and the defence against Fascism.

Hitler's accession to the German Chancellorship increased Victor's political publishing and he stopped subsidizing books without a political purpose. He published radical books that attacked fascism or capitalism but was less critical when it came to the Soviet Union. However, Gollancz did not publish everyone who was a communist sympathiser.

Humbert, also struck with the urgency to fight fascism, was more liberal and not a Communist. However, Gollancz would say, "I am a Communist because I am a Liberal" and once told Stephen Spender that he might retire into the country for a couple of years to write a huge book about the betrayal of liberalism by those who refused to accept that communism was its logical outcome.

By early 1937 *The New Statesman* and *Nation* attacked Gollancz for forcing writers to become communist sympathisers. This tension in his approach to writers can be seen In late October 1938 when Gollancz wrote to Leonard Woolf (who in 1931 became Joint Founder and Editor of *The Political Quarterly*). Gollancz asked if he would write for the Club a book on the defence by the Left of Western civilization against fascism, but with certain reservations about the Soviet Union and its dictatorship, saying:

"I see a future more and more dominated by lying propaganda, mass hysteria, violence, unscrupulousness and hatred: and I believe the most important thing of all is to preserve, so far as they can be preserved, tolerance, the open mind, freedom of thought and discussion, and so on. I have myself for many years held the view that these things (for which I have always cared more than for anything) were not ultimately possible in a capitalist society: and I have therefore been prepared - though with extreme reluctance - to defend the suppression of these things in the Soviet Union, on the ground that a socialist society cannot be brought into being except by means of a dictatorship, and that in this case, therefore, "the end justifies the means". I feel doubtful now whether that point of view was ever right: but whether it was or not, my own ideas on the subject have been altered by the new situation in which we find ourselves. I believe that here and now, without any compromise, these "liberal ideas" have got to be immediately defended and preserved. If this cannot be done, I see the extinction of everything decent in humanity."

However, when Leonard sent a manuscript Gollancz was afraid that the book's open criticism of Stalin's dictatorship would cause up to 10,000 Communists and near-Communists to resign from the Club. So the selectors wanted Leonard to make some alterations. Gollancz wrote to Leonard on 22 June, 1939; "We all feel that there are certain phrases in the book (I do not think more than half-a-dozen) which can very easily be dragged out of the context and used by reactionaries and, indeed, fascists as propaganda against the Soviet Union. We believe that these can be modified in such a way that your point is not put the smallest bit less strongly, while any possibility of distortion by fascists, etc., is obviated."

Leonard replied; "I must say that your letter rather astonishes me - not least that you now propose in any case to postpone publication of the book for over seven months....For the Soviet Union as a socialist state I have like you an affection (though not for Governments and governing cliques - which is a very different pair of shoes). It is just because of this that I think it essential to point out errors in policy which, as I explain in the book itself, seem to me fatal to the ultimate aim of socialism or communism."

Gollancz made excuses for the delay. "I see from your letter that, to put it bluntly, you don't believe me about the necessity in any case for postponement: but I assure you it is a fact."

Leonard was unimpressed and his next letter began: ""To put it bluntly", as you say, I do not believe in the necessity for an indefinite postponement of my book…As an author I am not interested in speculations regarding the imaginary influence which my book will have on international negotiations or the membership of the Left Book Club; I am interested in two things only: (1) that the book shall be published within a reasonable time and that it shall not therefore be indefinitely postponed until it is just out of date and all the edge taken off it, (2) that I am paid for my labours within a reasonable time ..." He ended by politely demanding to know the likely date of publication.

Gollancz then became upset that Leonard denied the effects that the book's publication might have on Anglo-Soviet negotiations or on Left Book Club membership. "I do not at all take the view that a book, when read by a quarter of a million people ... can have no effect on international relations. To admit such a thing would make nonsense of all my principles, as a publisher: and it seems to me also to make nonsense of a great part of the case for democracy . . . . I do happen to know my Left Book Club members."

And so they met on 24th July and spent three hours in difficult discussions as warmth increased on Gollancz's side of the room and coldness on Leonard's. However Leonard's book was published unaltered and unmodified and the two left as friends as Leonard recalled; "There was a slight cloud, slight tension in the room, but I am glad to remember that, before I went out, an absurd little incident entirely dispersed them. On the wall opposite to where I had been sitting was a picture which through the long, rather boring and exasperating, argumentative discussion I had frequently looked at with pleasure and relief. In gratitude to the painter, when I said good-night to Victor, I asked him who had painted it and added that I had got a great deal of pleasure by looking at it. I could not have said anything to give Victor more pleasure or more effectively relieve the tension, for the painter was his wife. I left the room, not under a cloud, but in a glow of good-will and friendship."

Ch 23 : THE WAR OF THE POETS (1936 – 1938)

On the opposite side many poets were completely in favour of the fascists. Most extreme of these was the original modernist, Ezra Pound.

In 1935 Pound heard the way that President Roosevelt used radio to rally public opinion so by 1936 Pound was broadcasting his own political and economic theories on the airwaves of Radio Rome. His comments were abrupt and fragmented like his poetry and prose, and they were extreme. He had defended Italy's invasion of Ethiopia and had been writing that "Jewspapers" had poisoned the world and that Jews was unable to accept civic responsibility because they had no nation of their own. He wrote that Jewish arrivistes were taking over "Jew York" and the "Jewnited" States which was enough to "justify all the Heil Hitlers, Goebbels and pogroms".

He attacked the Jews because he believed that they conspired to finance the war through usury and in *Canto XLV* Pound argued that medieval and Renaissance art and craft would not have been possible in a system of usury where "no picture is made to endure" as it is just made to "sell quickly."

However, his main criticism was that Monotheism was a Jewish development that had ended the pagan era. And he shared a belief in paganism with the Nazis. Yet despite all of these comments Pound denied being anti-Semitic, pointing out that he had many Jewish friends and claiming that the charge of anti-Semitism was a red herring as anti-Semitism was common in Europe and America at the time and that he also ranted against Christians and Americans.

In September 1938, Hitler and Neville Chamberlain signed their non-aggression pact. Pound saw the pact as the beginning of the end for America and England, that the international Jewish banking conspiracy would be exposed, and that Hitler and Mussolini were the two greatest statesmen alive.

Pound subscribed to fascism which T.S. Eliot saw as escapism and he saw the dangers of state control. Eliot wrote in defence of Pound that; "The views of any writer, if his mind develops and matures, will change or be modified by events," but Pound's views did not change and he was to be imprisoned in the USA in the 1940s for fascist broadcasting.

Eliot was also keen to save the reputation of writers whom he believed in and wrote in the preface of *One Way Song* that Wyndham Lewis had been falsely called a fascist; "As for Mr. Lewis's politics, I see no reason to suppose that he is any more of a 'fascist' or 'nazi' than I am. People are annoyed by finding that you are not on their side; and if you are not, they prefer you to surrender yourself to the other; if you can see the merits, as well as the faults, of the parties to which you do not belong, that is still worse. Anyone who is not enthusiastic about the fruits of liberalism must be unpopular with the Anglo-Saxon majority. So far as I can see, Mr. Lewis is defending the detached observer. The detached observer, by the way, is likely to be anything but a dispassionate observer; he probably suffers more acutely than the various apostles of immediate action."

In 1937 Eliot had been most concerned for his own future. He described himself in a nonsense poem to Virginia Woolf as "upper middle" class to put him in the solid, respectable group who he passed his business and social life with. By 1939 he wrote to Virginia that he was anxious and dissatisfied with the work that he was doing, and aware that he may never be able to write anything again. Also that a future race might come across the name of T.S. Eliot and wonder who he was.

As well as his self focus, Eliot also felt a "deep personal guilt and shame" at the non-aggression pact and that "national life seemed fraudulent." Yet despite his dislike of fascism in October 1938 he met with Pound and Lewis, in London.

Lewis painted Eliot in 1938 and Eliot remained his friend, believing that the critics had deliberately hurt Lewis's career. Eliot thought Lewis was a master of stylistic verse rather than poetry. "Lewis was independent, outspoken and difficult. Temperament and circumstances combined to make him a great satirist... His work was persistently ignored or depreciated, throughout his life, by persons of influence in the world of art and letters who did not find him congenial." He was "one of the few men of letters in my generation whom I shall call, without qualification, men of genius... Mr. Lewis is the greatest prose master of style of my generation – perhaps the only one to have invented a new style."

And in 1938, after a final trip to Berlin Lewis took back his earlier support of Hitler, became anti-Nazi and denied charges of anti-Semitism. However, some never forgave Lewis, despite his difference to Pound. His friendship with Pound remained and Lewis did a portrait in oils of Pound reclining and Pound helped Lewis by purchasing several drawings.

In *Letters from Iceland* 1937 W.H. Auden regretted that Lewis praised Hitler, making him an isolated intellectual;

> "There's Wyndham Lewis fuming out of sight,
> That lonely old volcano of the Right....
> We leave the martyr's stake at Abergwilly
> To Wyndham Lewis with a box of soldiers (blonde)
> Regretting one so bright should be so silly."

Other writers were more lenient on Lewis. Spender observed that; "Wyndham Lewis never supposed that he should become the mouthpiece of Hitler and the ideas put forward in Mein Kampf. He had in fact a rather supercilious attitude towards Hitler whom he patted (metaphorically) on the back for having expressed rather crudely certain ideas already in the mind of Wyndham Lewis." The fascist armies were "defending the past civilization of which they, the great artists, were the intellectual leaders."

In 1939 Lewis painted Spender again and although Spender disliked the portrait. Lewis was pleased with it and told Spender "It's as beautiful as a head by Raphael.". The painting was a visual representation of Dan Boleyn – "The tall melting, glowing young debutante, fixed in a stuck-still confusion, standing suffused with a hot maidenly bloom." "Downcast madonna-face, sensitively pained lips, blushing cheeks, long swan-neck, high wavy hair and the wild-eyed stare of his passionate velvet eyes."

And although Spender made excuses for Lewis he did not sign up with the rest of Lewis's friends. In 1939 Spender condemned Roy Campbell's *Flowering Rifle* as "ignoble sweepings of every kind of anti-Semitic and atrocity propaganda" and several passages made him feel physically sick. However, Campbell could no more see the perils of fascism than Spender could see the perils of Communism.

Other poets were even later than Lewis in retracting praise, failing to realise the brutality of Hitler's regime. In 1939 Osbert Sitwell still considered that; "Hitlerism is a true development of the English public school spirit. Certainly the descriptions of the concentration camps called into being by the present regimes, read in our newspapers very much like a word-picture of life at Eton."

His sister Edith Sitwell continued her own, more pressing, poetic wars. In 1936 she once more attacked Lewis in *Aspects of Modern Poetry* and called him a He-man with cave-man poetry. She said that Spender is just a refined version of another poet, Mr. W.J.Turner. What a bore Auden was and that "he has an able mind, but, unhappily he writes uninteresting poetry, or, at least, his poetry nearly always lacks interest. It is generally recognised that he is one of the four or five living poets worth quarrelling about. I can only reply that this is sheer nonsense."

Then in 1937 she left her publisher Duckworth for Victor Gollancz and published *I Live Under A Black Sun* in which a young country boy goes to the war. Lewis is in the book, as Henry Debingham. She had to change her original name for him from "Ratney Pierpoint," an amalgam of characters in Lewis' *The Apes of God* because Gollancz's lawyer H.F. Rubinstein saw a libel risk and suggested "Wyndham Lewis is a dangerous person. I speak from experience. I suggest, therefore, that no loophole should be allowed him to make trouble." However Edith's caricature of Lewis was mild and he was dismissive of "the old Jane's" latest work.

Ch 24 : OUTBREAK OF WAR (1939)

For me, dear reader, the War of the Poets ended when the real war began. Their battles and skirmishes were being replaced by greater battles that united both Right and Left in Britain.

On August 23rd 1939 the Russian and German foreign ministers signed the Molatov-Ribbentrop non-aggression pact. This meant that the Soviets didn't intervene when Hitler attacked Poland. Only when, on September 3rd, Germany ignored the ultimatum to pull out of Poland, did Britain and France declare war.

By December the Soviets invaded Finland and many resigned from Victor Gollancz's Left Book Club as Gollancz now found himself allied to the enemy and against friends.

At the outbreak of war Wyndham Lewis now supported Britain against the fascists in Spain and Germany, as did Roy Campbell. Campbell was now disabled and tried to get a job as an army Farrier and was put on coast watch, looking out for German submarines. He attacked those left wing poets of the Thirties, who urged others to fight Fascism during the Spanish Civil War but now, in 1939, took "soft jobs" or fled to America.

Cecil Day-Lewis enlisted in the Ministry of Information and Stephen Spender's health was judged too poor for service so he enlisted in the volunteer fire service. And W.H. Auden had gone to the USA before the war, where he stayed when war broke out and only returned after it finished.

James Joyce fled to Zurich from Nazi occupied France in 1940. Shortly afterwards he died following surgery for a perforated ulcer.

Edith Sitwell was also in France and returned to Renishaw where she lived with her brother Osbert and his lover David Horner. She knitted clothes for friends serving in the army. She continued to be critical and in 1940 thought Virginia Wolfe as a writer was "not an important artist at all." Virginia in turn had said that "the Sitwells, as a family, bore me."

Rebecca West criticised the government for appeasing Hitler and left-wing literary figures for their pacifism and support of Stalin. During the War she sheltered Yugoslav refugees in the spare rooms of her country manor, Ibstone House.

Pamela Frankau went into war work then left for America. After 9 years Frankau forgave West partly to honour the memory of the dead Humbert Wolfe. But the relationship remained difficult as Anthony West wrote a cruel satire on his mother which Frankau didn't condemn.

Sir William Rothenstein painted and drew R.A.F. servicemen at the Gloucestershire aerodromes. And Jessie Wolfe registered as a war painter

Rebecca West also visited Virginia Woolf and the experience was mutually disappointing and Virginia wrote about the visit; "Why this dilly-dallying with the world and the flesh? ... No, I don't think one makes much headway ..."

Virginia's and Leonard's home was destroyed in the Blitz. On 28th March 1941 Virginia committed suicide.

In the late 1930s Harold Nicholson was one of the first MP to take a stand to alert the country to the threat of fascism. He became parliamentary secretary and official censor in the Ministry of Information in the 1940s. His wife, Vita Sackville-West, worked to create the gardens at Sissinghust Castle.

T.S. Eliot's wife Vivienne was committed to a mental hospital in 1938 and remained there until she died. He never visited her. His new companion was Mary Trevelyan.

Robert Graves and Laura Riding moved to the United States. They parted in 1941 and Graves returned to England and Riding renounced poetry.

Siegfried Sassoon had a much wished for son in 1936 but separated from his wife Hester in 1945.

John Gawsworth served in the RAF as an aircraftsman in North Africa. As one of the Cairo poets, he made a more serious name for himself, being part of the Salamander group. He was regarded as one of the coming poets of the age but descended into alcoholism after the second world war.

Noel Coward ran the British propaganda office in Paris and also helped British intelligence to influence American opinion in favour of helping Britain

Nancy Cunard had predicted "events in Spain were a prelude to another war" and in the 1930s she worked to delivers supplies to Spanish refugees. During the war she was a translator in London helping the French Resistance.

BIBLIOGRAPHY

Ackroyd, Peter, "T.S.Eliot", Sphere Books, London 1985

Alexander, Peter, "Roy Campbell: A Critical Biography", Oxford University Press, 1982

Babington Smith, Constance, "John Masefield; A Life", Oxford University Press, 1978

Bagguley, Philip, "Harlequin in Whitehall", Nyala Publishing, London 1997

Bishop, Alan, "Chronicle of Friendship, Vera Brittain's Diary of the Thirites", Victor Gollancz, 1986

Brome, Vincent, "J.B. Priestley", Hamish Hamilton Ltd, London, 1988

Campbell, Roy, "The Georgiad", London 1931

Campbell, Roy, "Light On A Dark Horse", Penguin Books, 1971

Castle, Charles, "Noel", W H Allen, London, 1972

Church, Richard, "The Voyage Home", Heinemann Ltd, London 1964

Coward, Noel, "Autobiography", Methuen, London, 1986

Coward, Noel, "Chelsea Buns", Hutchinson & Co, London, 1925

Day-Lewis, Sean, "C.Day-Lewis: An English Literary Life", Unwin, London, 1982

Dudley Edwards, Ruth, "Victor Gollancz - A Biography", Victor Gollancz, London, 1987

Edmond, Lauris, "The letters of A.R.D. Fairburn", Oxford University Press 1981

Egremont, Max, "Siegfried Sassoon - A Biography", Picador, London, 2005

Elborn, Geoffrey, "Edith Sitwell: A Biography", Sheldon Press, London, 1981

Fielding, Daphne, "Emerald & Nancy - Lady Cunard and her Daughter", Eyre & Spottiswoode, London, 1968

Frankau, Pamela, "Ask Me No More", Heinemann, London 1958

Frankau, Pamela, "Fly Now Falcon", Riverside Press, New York 1935

Frankau, Pamela, "I Find Four People", Penguin, London 1938

Frankau, Pamela, "Pen to Paper", Doubleday, New York 1962

Frankau, Pamela, "The Willow Cabin", Heinemann, London 1949

Gawsworth, John, "An Unterrestrial Pity – Being Contributions Towards a Biography of the Late Pinchbeck Lyre by Orpheus Scrannel", London 1931

Glendinning, Victoria, "Edith Sitwell: A Unicorn Among Lions", Oxford University Press, 1983

Glendinning, Victoria, "Rebecca West - A Life", Weidenfeld and Nicolson, London, 1987

Gordon, Lyndall, "Eliot's New Life", Oxford University Press, 1989

Hart-Davis, Rupert, "George Moore Letter to Lady Cunard 1895-1933", Rupert Hart-Davis, London 1957

Hart-Davis, Rupert, "Letters of Max Beerbohm 1892-1956", Oxford University Press 1989

Holst, Imogen, "Gustav Holst - A Biography", Oxford University Press, 1988

Holst, Imogen, "Introduction", "Twelve Humbert Wolfe songs by Gustav Holst", Stainer & Bell, London 1969

Jameson, Storm, "Autobiography: Journey from the North, vol2", Virago, London 1984

Jenkins, Alan, "The Twenties", Heinemann Ltd, London, 1974

King, Bruce, "Robert Graves - A Biography", Haus Publishing, London, 2008

192

Lewis, Wyndham, "Blasting and Bombardiering - An Autobiography (1914-1926)", Calder an Boyars Ltd, London, 1937

Lewis, Wyndham, "The Apes of God", London 1930

Lewis, Wyndham, "One-Way Song", Methuen, London, 1960

Lewis, Wyndham, "Rude Assignment: An Intellectual Autobiography", Farnsworth, 1984

Mannin, Ethel, "Confessions and Impressions", 1930

Maugham, Robin, "Escape From The Shadows", Hodder and Stoughton, London, 1972

Meyers, Jeffrey, "The Enemy - A Biography of Wyndham Lewis", Routlege and Kegan Paul, London, 1980

Moeyes, Paul, "Siegfried Sassoon - Scorched Glory", St.Martin's Press, New York, 1997

Moorcroft Wilson, Jean, "Siegfried Sassoon - The Journey from the Trenches", Duckworth, London 2004

Hart-Davis, Rupert, "George Moore Letters To Lady Cunard 1895 – 1933", Rupert Hart-Davis, London, 1957

Morley, Sheridan, "A Talent To Amuse", Penguin, 1974

Pritchard, David, "James Joyce", Geddes & Grosset, Scotland 2001

Rothenstein, William, "Men & Memories 1972-1938", Chatto & Windus, London, 1978

Salter, Elizabeth, "Edith Sitwell", Oresko Books Ltd, London, 1979

Sassoon, Siegfried, "Poems of Pinchbeck Lyre", London 1931

Sitwell, Edith, "Taken Care Of: An Autobiography", Readers Union Hutchinson, London, 1966

Skelton, Robin, "The Memoirs of a Literary Blockhead", Macmillan, Canada, 1988

Smith, Rowland, "Lyric and Polemic: The Literary Personality of Roy Campbell", McGill Queen's University Press 1972

Spender, Stephen, "World Within World", Faber and Faber, London 1951

Stanfrod, Peter, "C Day-Lewis - A Life", Continuum, London 2007

Tytell, John, "Ezra Pound: The Solitary Volcano", Bloomsbury, 1987

Weldon, Fay, "Rebecca West", Penguin Books, 1985

West, Rebecca, "The Addict", Nash's Pall Mall Magazine, London1935

Williams-Ellis, Clough, "Architect Errant - The Autobiograpy of Clough Williams-Ellis", Golden Dragon Books, Glasgow 1980

Wolfe, Humbert, "Requiem" (London 1927, New York 1927)

Wolfe, Humbert, "The Uncelestial City" (London 1930, New York 1930)

Wolfe, Humbert, "ABC of the Theatre" (London 1932)

Wolfe, Jessie, "Last Portrait", (1941 unpublished)

Woolf, Virginia, "A Writer's Diary", Triad Grafton, London 1978

Woolf, Leonard, "Downhill All The Way: An Autobiography of the years 1919 – 1939", Hogarth Press, London 1968

Ziegler, Philip, "Osbert Sitwell: A Biography", Pimlico 1999

CHARACTERS + CHAPTERS

Auden, W.H. – poet (*1907–1973*) 9,13-14,17-18,20,22-24
Bennett, Arnold – writer, critic (*1867–1931*) 3,6,14-17
Campbell, Roy - poet (*1901–1957*) 3,8,10,16-18,22-24
Coward, Noel – playwright, actor (*1899–1973*) 6-7,11,18,24
Cunard, Nancy – poet, publisher (*1896–1965*) 3,7,10,12,15,18-19,24
Day-Lewis, Cecil – poet (*1904–1972*) 9,13-14,17-18,20,24
Eliot, T. S – poet, editor (*1888–1965*) 1,3,6,8-11,13-14,16-18,20,23-24
Frankau, Pamela – writer (*1908–1967*) 19,21,24
Garvin, Viola - journalist (*1898-1969*) 11,19,21
Gawsworth, John – poet (*1912-1970*) 17,24
Gollancz, Victor – publisher (*1893–1967*) 11,15,17,21-24
Graves, Robert - poet, soldier (*1895–1985*) 2-4,9-11,13,16-18,20,24
Hardy, Thomas – writer (*1840–1928*) 3,12,15,20
Holst, Gustav – composer (*1874–1934*) 12,15
Isherwood, Christopher – poet (*1904-1986*) 9,13
Joyce, James – writer (*1882-1941*) 1,6,14,18,21,24
Lawrence, T.E. - writer, soldier (*1888–1935*) 12,17,20
Lewis, Wyndham - poet, artist, soldier (*1882–1957*) 1,3,5-10,13,15-18,20-24
Manin, Ethel – writer, journalist (*1900-1984*) 11,15
Masefield, John – poet Laureate (*1878-1967*) 11,15
Monro, Harold – publisher (*1879-1932*) 1,11
Moore, George – writer (*1852–1933*) 3,6,10,15,19
Nicolson, Harold – writer, critic, civil servant (1886-1968) 16-17,24
Owen, Wilfred – poet, soldier (*1893-1918*) 2-3,11,13
Pound, Ezra – poet, critic (*1885–1972*) 1,3,6,10,18-19,23-24
Riding, Laura – writer, critic (*1901–1991*) 11,20,24
Rothenstein, Sir William – artist, writer (*1872–1945*) 1,5,11,18-19,24
Rutherston, Albert – artist, illustrator (*1881–1953*) 6,11,19,21
Sackville-West, Vita – poet (*1892–1962*) 10,14,16,18,24
Sassoon, Siegfried - poet, soldier (*1886–1967*) 2-5,8,11-13,17,20,24
Sitwell, Edith – poet, critic (*1887–1964*) 2-5,7-8,10-12,14-15,17-18,20,22-24
Sitwell, Osbert - poet, soldier (*1892–1969*) 2-5,7-8,10-11,17-20,22,24
Sitwell, Sacheverell – poet, soldier (*1897–1988*) 2-5,7-8,11,17-18,20
Spender, Stephen – poet (*1909–1995*) 8,13-14,16-18,22-24
Tennant, Stephen – artist (*1906-1987*) 12,17,20
Walton, William – composer (*1902-1983*) 3,7,10
West, Rebecca – poet (*1892–1983*) 1,10-12,14,17-19,21,24
Wolfe, Humbert – poet, critic, civil servant (*1885–1940*) 3,6,9,11-19,21,24
Wolfe, Jessie – artist (*1883- ?)* 11,15,19,21,24
Woolf, Leonard – writer, publisher (*1880–1969*) 4,6,10,13-14,18-19,22-24
Woolf, Virginia – writer, publisher, critic (*1882–1941*) 1,3-4,6-7,10,12,14,16,18-19,22-24

www.ingramcontent.com/pod-product-compliance
Lightning Source LLC
LaVergne TN
LVHW051631080426
835511LV00016B/2285